THE SECRET LIFE OF CATS

ROBERT DE LAROCHE • JEAN-MICHEL LABAT

AURUM PRESS

For Annick Bastit, so well named.
Affectionately.

R.L. and J.-M. L.

The authors and the editor wish to thank for their kindness:
Sylvie Dechuad
François Granges
Diane Harlé, archivist at the Department of Egyptian Antiquities,
Musée du Louvre
Dominique Kerforn
Jacques Laurent
Mme Peyret (Saint-Dyé-sur-Loire syndicat d'initiative)
Josette Rey-Debove, Alain Rey, and Le Robert dictionaries
Hervé Rougier
Marie-Fred Walravens

Elisabeth Rabeisen and the Musée Alésia (Alise-Sainte-Reine)
Sophie Fourny-Dargère and the Musée Alphonse-Georges Poulain
(Vernon)
The parish of the cathedral of Saint-Pierre (Poitiers)
Chantal Orgogozo and the Musée d'Aquitaine (Bordeaux)
Louis Causse and the Department of Architecture (Rodez)
Catherine Bellanger and the Musée du Louvre (Paris)
Chantal Rouquet and the Musée des Beaux-Arts et d'Archéologie
(Troyes)
The Municipal Corporation of Saint-Omer

Roland Mourer and the Musée d'Histoire Naturelle (Lyons)
Rosemarie Müller and the Musée du Chat (Riehen, Switzerland)
The Municipal Corporation of Paris (Department of Cultural Affairs)
Père Maurice and the parish of Sainte-Anne-de-Gassicourt (Mantes-la-
Jolie)
D'un chat l'autre (Biliothèque Internationale du Chat)
L'Agence Actis

The pictures appearing on the pages listed are reproduced by the kind
permission of the curators of the following museums:
pp. 17, 28, 34, 35, 37, 38, 85, 98, 99, 104, 106: Musée du Louvre, Paris
p. 8: Illustration by Jacques Nam, with the permission of Jacqueline
Cuzelin-Guerret
pp. 18, 19, 27: Musée Guimet d'Histoire Naturelle, Lyons
pp. 50, 96: Musée Alphonse-Georges Poulain, Vernon
pp. 15, 32, 48, 63, 109, 110, 115: Musée du Chat, Riehen, Switzerland
p. 31: Musée d'Aquitaine, Bordeaux
p. 40: Musée Municipal, Alise-Sainte-Reine
p. 46: Musée des Beaux-Arts et d'Archéologie, Troyes
pp. 72, 90: Department of Cultural Affairs, Municipal Corporation/City
Council of Paris
p. 91: Photo by Aldo.

First English edition published in Great Britain 1993 by
Aurum Press Limited, 25 Bedford Avenue, London WC1B 3AT

Published by arrangement with Casterman, s.a.

A CIP catalogue record for this book is available from the British Library

ISBN 1 85410 508 6

1 3 5 7 9 10 8 6 4 2
1997 1999 2001 2000 1998

Editors: Giampiero Caiti, Philippe Demoulin, assisted by Carine Herman
Design: Sandra Brys
Typeset by Clive Dorman & Co.
Printed in Spain.

THE SECRET LIFE OF CATS

ROBERT DE LAROCHE • JEAN-MICHEL LABAT

AURUM PRESS

The cat went here and there
And the moon spun round like a top,
And the nearest kin of the moon,
The creeping cat, looked up.
Black Minnaloushe stared at the moon,
For, wander and wail as he would,
The pure cold light in the sky
Troubled his animal blood.
Minnaloushe runs in the grass
Lifting his delicate feet.
Do you dance, Minnaloushe, do you dance?
When two close kindred meet,
What better than call a dance?

W.B. Yeats (1865-1939),
from *The Cat and the Moon*.

I am particularly happy that this book has been translated into English, because I think that the seeds of my fascination with cats were sown at the French Cinémathèque, where I acquired most of my knowledge of English from watching British and American films without subtitles. Cats often featured in the films. I remember, for instance, the lovely Leslie Caron singing — with a devastating broken accent — to a bewildered Fred Astaire:

C-A-T spells cat

R-A-T spells rat

Although the cat can catch the rat

The rat can't catch the cat

It was a nice, easy way to learn English...

A few years later, in Normandy, where I live most of the time when I'm not in Paris, I heard that a neighboring farm had an unwanted kitten. I went to the farmhouse and asked if I could have it. The old lady I spoke to evidently felt I should be warned: "Oh, my boy! But it's a black cat. And they're bad luck, nobody wants it."

Undeterred, I said that I wanted the kitten anyway. And off I went with little Cleo in my arms. My whole family fell under her spell and we soon found her a husband, Pasha, who came from a Parisian cemetery, and they had a son, Bidule. It was the beginning of years of happiness for us.

But there was one thing that continued to puzzle me: how was it possible that an animal that gave such joy had been looked upon as a devil in past centuries?

My curiosity soon led me to do some research, and that's how I came to write my first book on cats, ten years ago. What did I learn, as I indulged myself by investigating the intricate love-hate relationship between cats and men? Mostly that a passion for cats is a strange and delicious poison for which, fortunately, there is no antidote. Once you have looked into a cat's eyes, you fall under a spell.

That's what happened to me, and with all my heart I wish you the same good fortune.

Robert de Laroche

A   D R E A M   O F   T H E   F I R S T   C A T

Share with me a recurrent dream. The scene is a desert oasis, dark and silent under a star-filled sky. The time is the very dawn of mankind, the place some ancient Eastern land. Persia? Egypt? I don't know. All that I can recall is the sickly smell, the searing heat of the sand, and the quality of the silence, occasionally broken by the rustling of the wind in the foliage of the palm groves. There are no wild cats on the prowl tonight, I can tell, for my sharp sense of smell, attuned to every potential threat, receives no warning signal.

Then, suddenly, my skin crawls, my muscles tense, the blood beats in my temples, my heart is in my mouth. I sense the approach of an unknown visitor, its paws stealthily treading the sand. An animal, yes, but which? Is it attracted by the prospect of food, or by my presence? It draws nearer and I can make out the glow of two green spots of light. The creature is feline, but very small....

With a trembling hand I toss the left-overs of my meal toward it. It makes as if to escape, then there is silence. It waits, then slowly advances. The offering is accepted. I move forward, filled with fear and curiosity. I know its fear is as intense as my own, its curiosity even greater. How long, I wonder, will it take us to bridge the few yards that separate us?

Which of us took the initiative and tamed the other first — man or beast? The thought intrigues me, and how I would love to have been that Neolithic man who first encountered the cat, that extraordinary blend of wildness and gentleness.

Was I the actor in this crucial scene, in some former life? Is this why I feel compelled to investigate the cat in detail? Not simply to retrace its history (which has already been done many times), but to explore, with the assistance of Jean-Michel Labat's remarkable photographs, some unfamiliar aspects of its personality, its central role in mythology — half-divinity, half-devil — its unique relationship with man.

The wonderful thing about the cat is the way in which, when one of its mysteries is laid bare, it is only to reveal another. The essential enigma always remains intact, a sphinx within a sphinx within a sphinx, like one of those Russian dolls.

My own belief is that the cat was created to encourage us to dream. I even suspect it knows the limits of our imagination and plays on them, inspiring us to attribute to it a thousand and one marvels, thus adding to its mystery.

Like poets, cats lead us along the margins of the everyday, visible world. By following in their footsteps we can slip behind the looking glass, to find, as often as not, that the reflection in the mirror is our own image. He who knows the cat surely understands himself a little better.

ROBERT DE LAROCHE

MYTHIC ORIGINS

In creation myths, the cat is universally linked to the mother goddesses and to the stars of Day and Night. Its mythology is also linked to that of the lion, which, once common in Egypt, was becoming increasingly rare when the theologians of Heliopolis were codifying their accounts of the complex Egyptian pantheon. It seems possible that the story of the taming of the lioness Sekhmet, who was transformed into the gentle cat Bastet, has a literal parallel in the virtual extinction of the lion and the simultaneous proliferation of the cat.

Those with imaginations claim that the cat came from Atlantis, or was a creation of Egyptian veterinarians. Cats are not mentioned in the Bible, except for a brief reference thought to stem from a mistranslation. The Muslims believe the cat first appeared on Noah's Ark when, pestered by numerous rats infesting the boat, the old man asked God's advice. He was ordered to hit the lion's muzzle, causing the beast to sneeze forth the first pair of cats. Mohammed is supposed to have bestowed upon the cat one of its remarkable abilities. One day, when the prophet was preparing himself for prayer he found that his cat, Muezza, was sleeping on his robe; unwilling to disturb the creature, the prophet tore off the sleeve on which she rested. On his return, Muezza expressed her gratitude with a deep bow. In order

"Time spent with cats is never wasted." Colette, Les Vrilles de la Vigne (The Tendrils of the Vine).

to acknowledge this display of exquisite politeness, Mohammed granted to the cat and others like it the gift of always landing on their feet.

In Buddhism, which traces its origins back to antiquity, the cat occupies an equivocal position, attributed to an incident that took place at the time of the Buddha's death. All the animals gathered, weeping, around the sacred remains; only the snake and the cat remained dry eyed. To make matters worse, the cat pounced on a rat that was drinking the oil from a lamp, and proceeded to eat it.

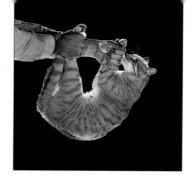

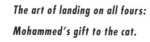

The art of landing on all fours:
Mohammed's gift to the cat.

The Khmers believed that the first tortoiseshell cat was created in a magic ritual performed by an old sage, and sprang from the menstrual blood of a young goddess born of a lotus flower. The connection with this powerfully symbolic plant indicates a link with the great Indo-European mother-Goddesses. The mythology of Greece and Rome followed that of Egypt in attributing the cat's origins to the divinities of the moon, Artemis and Diana.

Under the influence of Christianity, Western mythology replaced the duality of sun and moon with the Manichaean conflict of good versus evil. Thus the dog is a creation of God and the cat the work of the devil. While the cat's body may have been made by God, its head was certainly the devil's creation. Another version, however, holds that the cat is privileged with knowing the path back to the Garden of Eden. Amid the general misery that accompanied the expulsion of Adam and Eve and their children from Paradise, the cat was the only one to make a note of the route. Touched by the tears of Jacob, the third son of the First Parents, he led the little boy to the gates of Heaven. The Angel of Light, guardian of the gates, was moved by the sincerity of the child and the courage with which he and his cat had crossed the vast deserts, and offered his visitors a fruit. From that time on, it is said, there is always somewhere in the world a child and a cat who know the secret of the way back to the Garden of Eden. As the French artist Léonor Fini so gracefully expresses it: "Our companion the cat is the warm, furry, whiskered and purring reminder of a lost paradise."

15

IN THE CAT'S FOOTSTEPS

Ten thousand years before Christ, man exchanged his nomadic existence for a settled one, began to cultivate the earth and to tame various animals. Cultivation brought with it rodents, and these in turn attracted predators. From the outset it seems likely that the cat became what zoologists now classify as a "wild visitor," living at some distance from the Neolithic settlements while bene-fitting from their presence. As yet, excavation of these sites yields no evidence to show that the domes-tication of the cat — man's control of its feeding and reproduction — had begun.

The earliest known cat remains associated with human settlement were found on the site of Jericho in Palestine and date from 6700 B.C. Later traces, dating back to 2000 B.C., were found during the excavations of Harappa in the Indus Valley. There is some doubt in each case, since not enough bones have been found to allow for measurement of the skull, which, being more developed in the domestic cat than the wild one, is crucial to accurate identification. Cat remains dating from nearly 5000 B.C. have also been found in Cyprus; these were almost certainly animals imported from the Orient. An ivory statue of a recumbent cat, dating from 1700 B.C., was found on the site of Lachisch in Israel, while a terracotta cat's head of about the same date was discovered on the Minoan

Headdress of the god Bes. Earthenware. Late Period, Egypt.

site of Palaikastro on the coast of Crete.

There is a theory that the cat came to Egypt, already domesticated, from Pakistan or Persia. This would have been the Asiatic *Felis ornata*, which is still found wild in Iran and Pakistan. However, this theory ignores the existence of another species, the *Felis libyca*, or "gloved cat," which is a native of the Libyan desert and is still found in Egypt. Unlike the European wildcats of today, these two species allow humans to approach them. A third possibility is that the domestic cat is a product of interbreeding between these two species, possibly with a contribution from a third, the *Felis chaus*, or jungle cat, also native to Egypt.

One tradition suggests that cats had been domesticated in Egypt as early as the Third and Fourth Dynasties, *c.* 2600 B.C., the time of the pyramid-building pharaohs Zoser, Cheops, Chephren, and Mycerinus. Their titanic monuments are thought to have been built by a huge workforce of Nubian slaves. The gloved cats that frequented their settlements in what is now the Sudan may have followed them to the sites of Saqqarah and Giza. At first subsisting on the fish of the Nile and the birds that nested among the papyrus reeds, the cats would soon have attached themselves to the local peasants, protecting their granaries and ridding their homes of the various rodents that infested them.

The earliest concrete evidence of the existence of cats in the Ancient Empire dates from the Fifth Dynasty (*c.* 2500 B.C.); the effigy of a cat wearing a collar was discovered in the tomb of Ti at Saqqarah. The Eleventh Dynasty (*c.* 2100 B.C.) yields further proof of

Cats were mummified in great quantities in Egypt, some being killed for the purpose.

18

the cat's domestication, with mention of the nickname "She-cat" for a court personage. The cult of the goddess Bastet emerged in the following dynasty, *c.* 2000 B.C.

From the time of the New Empire and the Eighteenth Dynasty (*c.* 1500 B.C.), the cat assumed an important role in the religious and daily life of Egypt, as shown by Theban tomb frescoes, sarcophagi, papyri, and many common objects in daily use. For example, one tomb painting on display in the British Museum shows the use of trained cats to catch birds; a hunter in a boat with his family aims a snake-shaped stick while his tabby cat has seized three birds, one in her mouth, one with her forepaws, and one with her hind paws. The tomb of Nakht (Eighteenth Dynasty) is decorated with a cat eating a fish under the chair of the scribe's wife. In the tomb of Menna, a cat digs out a kingfisher's nest watched by an *ichneumon*, or Pharaoh's rat. From the Nineteenth and Twentieth Dynasties there are papyrus paintings of an episode from *The Book of the Dead* relating the exploits of the Great Cat. Further evidence is provided by the *ostraca* (fragments of pottery on which the tomb-painters amused themselves with satirical sketches and pictures). These show the degree to which cats had established themselves as pets, frequently depicting them as the subject of fables illustrating the "upside-down world"; we see them acting as guardians of geese, or servants of royal mice.

The earliest known cat sarcophagus dates from the Eighteenth Dynasty and comes from Saqqarah. Sculpted in limestone, it shows several feline effigies surrounding the goddesses Isis and Nephthys — the

animals are pictured seated upright and mummified before an offertory. The inscriptions reveal that the sarcophagus contained the body of a female cat belonging to one of the high priests of Memphis.

The custom of mummifying and interring cats reached its height when the cult of Bastet came to the fore under the pharaohs of Bubastis (*c.* 950 B.C.). Most of the surviving mummies date from the subsequent Saite period (Twenty-sixth Dynasty, 664–525 B.C.), the first Persian conquest (525–404 B.C.) and the Greco-Roman period (332 B.C.–395 A.D.). We know from the writings of Herodotus that as late as 500 B.C. the cat was almost unknown in Greece, where weasels,

the domestic cat, confirmed by works of art such as the Polopoulos bas-relief (*c.* 510–500 B.C.), depicting a confrontation between a cat and a dog. Valued for its usefulness and its beauty, the cat pursued its route into Europe by way of Italy. The evidence of tomb frescoes, a mosaic from Pompeii and writers such as Cicero and Pliny the Elder show the degree to which the cat became integrated into Roman society, as a familiar companion, a children's pet and *genius loci*. Its independent nature appealed to the Romans so much that in the second century B.C. a cat was depicted at the foot of a statue of the Goddess of Liberty in a temple in Rome.

For a long time some writers maintained that cats were unknown to the Gauls and barely known to the Celts, in whose lands they had appeared only briefly at the time of the Roman conquest, and that they did not become established in northern Europe until the turn of the tenth century. But this theory overlooks various Gallo-Roman sculptures in which cats appear. Moreover, the animals could easily have crossed the sea to France on merchant ships from Egypt delivering cargoes to Marseilles; after jumping ship there they could have made their way north along the valleys of the Rhône and Saône.

Cat remains have been found on the sites of Roman villas as far apart as Hungary and England. Others have been discovered in the burial pits of a Gallo-Roman villa in southwest France, while a Merovingian village in the north has yielded evidence of cats and dogs living alongside men. Cats seem to have been quite common in Saxon England, where numerous skeletons dating from the early seventh

ferrets, and grass snakes — less attractive creatures — watched over the crops. Then the Greeks began to mount covert expeditions to steal cats from Egypt, where, if caught, they risked severe punishment because of the sacred status of the animals. A flourishing trade later developed, with Phoenician and Greek merchants selling Oriental cats to private individuals, often at exorbitant prices.

Aesop, Aristophanes, and Callimachus provide much valuable information on the establishment of

century clearly indicate that the cat was already well established as a domestic animal.

In about 945 A.D. the Welsh king Hywel Dda (or Howell the Good) passed a series of laws aimed at protecting the cat and establishing its value for compensation if killed or stolen, which was based on its ability as a mouser:

The price of a kitten before it can see is one penny. If it has caught a mouse, its value is raised to twopence, and afterwards to fourpence. If anyone should steal or slay the cat guarding the royal granary, he shall be compelled either to forfeit an ewe or as much wheat as will cover the cat when suspended by its tail.

Though obviously not as valuable as his best mouser, the king's pet cat was also worth considerably more than anyone else's, being valued at one pound.

While Hywel Dda's code was intended principally to prevent the theft and torture of cats, it was also very probably meant to halt the widespread practice of killing them for their coats, which were highly prized by furriers. However, it was not until the fourteenth century, according to *The Book of Trades*, that a distinction was made between the trade in "skins of wild cats" and those of "the private cats called hearth or household cats."

In addition to the many other mysteries and conjectures surrounding the cat, its very name is an enigma. The origin of the word "cat" continues to provoke almost as much disagreement among linguists as is aroused among zoologists by the puzzle of the domestic cat's geographical and genetic origins.

The ancient Egyptians referred to the cat by the onomatopoeic *myeou* or *miou*, a phonetic transcription of the animal's hieroglyph that depicted it seated in profile. Certain funerary inscriptions give the term *techau*, indicating a female cat; according to Pierre Larousse, the Coptic word for cat was *chau*. Other lexicographers trace the origin of the word "pussy" to the Egyptian Pasht, one of the names for Bastet; it has also been suggested the French *matou* — tomcat — is an anagram of Atum (spelled Atoum in French), an Egyptian sun deity linked to the cat.

When Herodotus refers to the cat in his *Histories*, he calls it *ailuros*, and this Greek word survives in the English "ailurophobia," meaning the excessive fear of cats.

Before cats were imported into Greece, rodents were dealt with by various other animals such as stone martens, polecats, and weasels, known as *gale*. By the third century B.C. this meaning of the word had been expanded to cover cats. In texts from the second century A.D. the term *katoikidios*, "of the household,

domestic," was often used in conjunction with *gale*, referring to the domestic cat.

In Latin there was a similar shift in meaning: *felis*, which originally meant wildcat, weasel, etc., came to mean cat, Cicero being the first to use it in this precise sense in the first century A.D. *Felis* is of course the origin of our word "feline," but "cat" and the French *chat* come from *cattus*, later *catus*, a word of uncertain origin, first used in the low Latin of Palladius in the fourth century A.D.

Why these two Latin alternatives, *felis* and *cattus*? And why did the latter supplant the former? One unproven hypothesis claims that *cattus* replaced *felis* when the domestic cat of the East was introduced to Rome. This is supported by the likelihood that the word *cattus* is of North African or Middle Eastern origin. The Nubian for cat (or weasel) was *kadis*, in Berber it is *kadiska*, in Syrian *qato*, in Arabic *qitt*. The role of the domestic cat as an alternative ratcatcher to the weasel may play some part in the use of *cattus*; the Latin for weasel is *catta*, thought to originate in the Nubian *kadis*. This derivation is favored by today's linguists in preference to the explanation to be found in a twelfth-century *Bestiary* or Catalogue of Animals: "The vulgar call her Catus the Cat because she catches things (*acaptura*) while others say that it is because she lies in wait (*captat*), that is because she 'watches'."

While the common people may have used "cat," the contemporary scholarly word for cat was *musio* (from *mus*, *muris*, meaning mouse), or *murilegus* (mouse taker). But whatever its origin, it was *cattus* that prevailed, reappearing in numerous guises: *gato*

(Portuguese and Spanish), *gatto* (Italian), *chat* (French), *kochka* (Russian), *Katze* or *Kater* (German), and, of course, our own word "cat."

Like many animals, the cat has also enriched our everyday language where it appears in a whole array of proverbs and metaphors. Many of these are no longer in common usage, as for example "to turn the cat in the pan," which means either "to make black white" or, by extension, "to change sides." Others testify to some well-known characteristic of the animal: its calculating prudence ("wait to see which way the cat jumps"), its alleged inscrutability ("to make a cat laugh"), its vigilance ("when the cat's away, the mice will play"), or its penchant for having some sport with its prey before killing it ("playing cat and mouse"). As everyone knows, "a cat in gloves catches no mice," i.e., restraint and caution ("pussy-footing") achieves nothing, while "there is more than one way to skin a cat." Some of these sayings have been transmuted over the centuries; Shakespeare's "Who is it but loves good liquor. 'Twill make a catte speake" (*The Tempest*, II ii), recalls the phrase "enough to make a cat laugh," but who remembers the "adage" of *Macbeth*'s "Letting 'I dare not' wait upon 'I would', Like the poor cat i' the adage" (I vii)? In fact, this is derived from a thirteenth-century parable of the cat "who would eat fish but would not wet her feet." A "cat's-paw" is a person used as a tool by another, and harks back to the sixteenth-century tale of the monkey who used a cat's foot or paw to rake chestnuts out of the fire. The noise of tomcats at night is aptly described as "caterwauling," and their activity gives us "catting" i.e., going after the opposite sex (although "cat-house," a nineteenth-century term for brothel, appears to derive from a fortified moveable structure used by besiegers to protect themselves when approaching a fortress). However, "a good wife and a good cat are best at home" and anyone who has ever had to transport a cat, particularly if the destination is the vet's office, will know the perils of "letting the cat out of the bag," just as anyone who has foolishly attempted to quiet one with lofty human authority will know that "a cat may look at a king."

Always alert, even when fast asleep, the watchful cat was believed by the Egyptians to be one of the privileged guardians of the doors of the night and the kingdom beyond. Lions and dog-faced baboons stood at the frontier, while the cat mounted constant guard in the deepest shadows, knife at the ready to slice off the head of Apep, the Serpent of Evil, as described in several passages from the Book of the Dead and on various steles.

The sacred texts' description of the Great Cat or Great Tomcat makes him sound like a humorous creature, with enormous rabbit's ears, a tiger-striped coat, and smiling face. Belying his appearance, however, the divine cat has a heroic role in a crucial episode of the night voyage of the divine boat, a drama played out each night after Ra, the sun, has completed his daytime journey across the twelve regions of Egypt. At six in the evening the sun sinks into sleep and passes the gates of the underworld, accompanied by a cortège of the righteous dead. In Amenta, the kingdom of the dead, Ra, now helpless and an easy prey for demons, passes the night hours. At the eighth hour Apep, an emanation of Seth, a slippery and malevolent serpent, tries to stop the divine boat by drinking the water that runs beneath the vessel. But the Great Cat appears, apparently an embodiment of the sleeping divinity, since the texts present him as follows:

I am Atum, the divine cat of Heliopolis. O righteous dead who struggled against the Spirit of Evil in life, I will put far hence from you these evil spirits, into Amanta, for I am Atum of the Spaces of Heaven, Atum of the Creation and the End of the World.

An invincible guardian, the Great Cat cuts off the head of Apep and the divine boat continues on its course, hailed by the resurrected who, as the text has it, give vent to approving "meows." At the twelfth hour the sun is reborn, in the form of Khepri the scarab beetle. This struggle of light and shade was reenacted each night, an eternal conflict that mirrored the equilibrium of the universe.

This power of the cat over the forces of darkness is shown in statuary, where the protective role of feline effigies can be linked to that of the sphinx. Egyptian priests thought to confer on certain statues a life of their own by depicting them with open eyes and mouths. The stone, touched by the breath of life, thus possessed "a heart and a *ka* (life force)," and the living statue — the word is a translation of the Egyptian *shespankh*, meaning sphinx — drew into itself a measure of divine power.

Like the lion, the cat had the power to purge the atmosphere of evil exhalations, both in temples and in homes, where it kept particular vigil over sleepers in the same way as the Great Cat protected Ra. The fact that the Egyptians should have chosen as Guardian of Sleep an animal that spends around 70 percent of its existence asleep and dreams for up to four hours each day is an indication that the study of cat behavior was really far advanced in the Pharaonic period!

different animal, as for example in the case of the cat mummy found to contain a frog. One can imagine the priests at Bubastis, guardians of the sacred cats, or in the other temples where Bastet was worshipped, developing a trade in mummies that the devoted pilgrims then offered to the goddess in the hope of future favors or to thank her for a favor already granted. Perhaps the demand for cat cadavers outran supply, and this led to the use of cheaper substitutes. Nevertheless, when the temple of Bast at Beni-Hassan was excavated in the nineteenth century, it yielded 300,000 embalmed and mummified cats. These were shipped to Liverpool and Manchester, where they were sold for fertilizer.

Researchers have also discovered elongation and fracture marks in the cervical vertebrae of some mummified cats, proving that the animals had been deliberately killed. Was this a case of ritual sacrifice or, more prosaically, was it a question of ensuring an adequate supply of raw material for the pilgrims' mummies? In the absence of documentation, the uncertainty persists, as does the fascination and puzzlement inspired by what Champfleury so aptly describes as "those curious mummies which, in their extreme thinness and elongation, seem like bottles of precious wine surrounded by tresses of straw."

This role as guardian of the threshold between this world and the next, as necessary to sleepers as to the souls of the dead, has been assigned to the cat across the ages, and in diverse civilizations. Those who know the animal's role in Egyptian mythology cannot remain unmoved by the presence of such large numbers of cats in cemeteries all over the world.

OPPOSITE *Egyptian cat in bronze.*

"Cats which have died are taken to Bubastis, where they are embalmed and buried in sacred receptacles," writes Herodotus. There were several other cat necropolises at Saqqarah, Beni-Hassan, Stabl Antar, and it was supposed until recently that cats that died, whether in temples or in private households, were embalmed, mummified — some being placed in sarcophagi — and then buried in one of the cemeteries consecrated to the animal. However, new discoveries have shed fresh light on this mystery, for examinations of several cat mummies have revealed surprising contents—not a whole cat, but only a few fragments, sometimes just a bone, or even a quite

examples have come to light throughout the Roman world. Several steles found in France depict similar themes and a catalogue of Gallo-Roman bas-reliefs lists at least five. Three of them show a little girl seated in a niche, holding a cat in her arms. On one of these steles, found in Lyons in 1900, the child, dressed in a bonnet and a long tunic, strokes the animal. A rather different representation appears on a stele discovered in Dijon in the seventeenth century. Here a boy stands upright, a whip in his right hand, holding a cat in the crook of his left elbow. But the most touching image from the Gallo-Roman era is surely the so-called stele of Laetus, found in the Roman wall of Bordeaux in 1831. A little girl holds a kitten that is drawing itself away from a cock that pecks the tip of its tail. This vivid scene seems to support the theory that it was customary for the Romans and Gauls, who buried their children along with their toys, also to represent them on memorials accompanied by their pets. It's hard to resist the notion that the cat, as *genius loci*, was associated with the spirit of the dead, and thus his presence, as a sort of ultimate traveling companion, at the infant's side, was the guarantee of a safe journey into the other world.

Visitors to the Garden of Rest in the village of Old Cleeve, in Somerset, England, will be surprised to find there a fifthteenth-century tomb with a man lying down, his feet resting on a cat, whose paws are placed on a mouse. It is the most harmonious scene imaginable, suggesting the certainty of peaceful sleep, filled with happy dreams throughout eternity... except, of course, for the mouse.

In Greece, where its role was that of a children's pet, the cat seems to have been linked with its protégé even after death, as is shown in the funerary stele of Salamine (420 B.C.), which depicts a young child and a cat. This Greek image is an isolated case, but later

Funerary stele of Laetus.
Limestone, late first or early
second century A.D.

I am born of the divine She-cat, conceived beneath the sycamore of the enclosure by the seed come from on high, that my divinity may never be denied... I am born of the sacred She-cat, but I am also become a son of the Sun... born of the She-cat, I am the chief, the son of the She-cat, the double-guide, who will for his mother eternally remain the little one saved by the She-cat.

Thus does Osiris express himself in the Book of the Dead, indicating the feline nature of his divine mother, Nut, goddess of heaven.

Since earliest times, the cat, at once Pupil of Ra and Eye of Horus, fruitful warmth of the sun and fertility linked to the moon, has been associated with maternity. The Egyptians were certainly struck by cats' reproductive capacity, the legendary nature of which Plutarch would subsequently emphasize:
It is said in fact that this animal makes one baby, then two, then three, then four, then five, and thus as many as seven at a time, such that in all it can go as far as twenty-eight, a number equal to that of the days of the moon.

As Egyptian theology evolved and was modified, the sacred She-cat would be particularly identified with Isis, Hathor, and Sekhmet the lioness, whose benign aspect was represented by Bastet, the cat-goddess who sprang from the Eye of the Sun. Initially, Bastet's significance lay in her lioness/She-cat duality, and it was only with the full blossoming

Cat playing with her kitten. Egyptian bronze.

of her cult, towards the end of the New Kingdom (which lasted from 1540–1070 B.C.) and during the Third Intermediate Period and the Saitic era (*c.* 1069–525 B.C.) that she was definitively associated with the image of the She-cat. When Pharaoh Sheshank I, founder of the Twenty-second Dynasty *c.* 950 B.C., chose as his capital the city called Bubastis in Greek (Tell Basta in modern Egyptian), Bastet became the greatest divinity of the kingdom, as Bubastis was the center of her largest cult. Thenceforth, the goddess had her own temple at Per Bast (House of Bastet), near Zagazig in the Nile delta. Bubastis is today no more than a field of ruins, and it is impossible to imagine the splendor of the temple described by Herodotus, its immensity, the harmony of its porticoes shaded with trees, and its exceptional location, on the overhanging shore of an island forming two arms of the Nile. "Other temples may be larger, or have cost more to build, but none is a greater pleasure to look at."

Like all the temples of Pharaonic Egypt, Per Bast was open to the faithful only during religious festivals; on other days the priests and priestesses of Bastet celebrated the cult of the divine mother in deepest secret. In the second month of the season of Inundation, the Temple was a place of pilgrimage attracting hundreds of thousands of visitors each year for the Feast of Bastet. These celebrations, to which the people of the countryside journeyed by boat, took place in a climate of jubilation and freedom. The passengers, dancing to the sound of singing and castanets, insulted the people they saw on the banks, while the women provoked them by hitching up their skirts and shouting out obscenities — this feigned aggression was, no doubt, a means of reenacting the myth of Sekhmet the Violent, transported down the Nile on a boat to become the gentle Bastet of the south, and dispensing fertility on her way. The ceremonies at Bubastis, accompanied by sacrifices, were

Madonna with cat. Alabaster.

St. Omer Cathedral, France.

Talisman for a happy pregnancy. Egyptian earthenware.

an occasion for libations that Herodotus describes as involving "a greater consumption of wine than throughout all the rest of the year."

What, then, was Bastet's status? Goddess of music, of dance and of *joie-de-vivre*, she was at first the protectress and nurse of the royal children, then goddess of maternity, and finally protectress of the entire Egyptian people. She was to become a goddess of immense prestige, as is borne out by the various epithets accorded her on temple steles, parchments, and sculptures. Bastet was "Lady of Heaven," "Lady of the Casket, initiated into the mysteries of Atum," "the White One, nurse of the Great Castle," "Great Conjuress of the Casket," "Mistress of the Oudjat Eye."

Numerous talismans and amulets in blue-green earthenware survive, showing a cat (sometimes with a woman's head), her breasts swollen, surrounded by kittens, often in conjunction with a figure of the god Bes, attendant at births and officer of nursing duties. Some of these talismans were worn around the neck, others, mounted on poles, no doubt played a ritual part during childbirth. All attest to the crucial role of Bastet during the various phases of maternity. She protected pregnant women, watched over the gestation period, aided labor, suckled babies, and acted as nurse. Some statuettes show a cat lying

This type of amulet put mother and child under the protection of Bastet.

down, feeding her young ones or watching over their games, or, still standing, accompanied by her three attributes, the sistrum, the basket, and the aegis. The sistrum (a sort of primitive tambourine), when shaken, would ward off evil spirits from the beds of young mothers; the cane basket was the attribute of midwife-priestesses; as for the aegis, a medallion of leonine or feline form placed on the goddess' breast, this was to reinforce her protective power. The significance of the term "Great Conjuress of the Casket" remains unclear, but it was probably linked to a protection rite of the child Horus, before the afore-mentioned casket became the attribute of the magicians and doctors of Bastet, for the goddess was likewise their patroness. Perhaps, as has been suggested, this casket contained magical herbs or talismans intended to aid newborn children. From nurse "in the Great Castle" (i.e. in Ra's stronghold), then that of Pharaoh, his representative on earth, Bastet became the nurse of all the children of Egypt. A papyrus from Fayoum informs us that, among the orders of the priestesses of Bastet, there existed a denomination or affiliation called "Nurse of the She-cat." Babies and infants were not the only ones to benefit from the goddess' indulgence; her protection continued as far as the adolescence of the young ones she had, symbolically, brought into the world.

Cat silhouettes were tattooed on children's arms, to evoke the goddess' redemptive presence, and the temple magicians even injected infants with a few drops of blood from sacred cats, to protect them from epidemics or harmful influences. During the Libyan and Kush eras, numerous children were given names that incorporated that of Bastet, such as Nes-Bastet ("the one of Bastet") or even Djed-Bastet-iouef-ankh ("Bastet said 'let him live'").

Symbols have a habit of outlasting the beliefs of those who created them. Papyri showing cat-featured Nut in the enclosure of the sacred sycamore, a serpent's head crushed under her right paw, now seem to prefigure images of the Christian era—of the Virgin Mary with the dragon beneath her heel, or of the Madonna with a Cat, an image beloved by medieval artists. When the Christian Mother inherited the attributes of Isis and Bastet, she also inherited their symbols.

Just as the cat was a guardian of the threshold for the Egyptians, so it seems to have been considered as a *genius loci*, or household spirit, by the Gallo-Romans. A discovery made in 1937 at Alise-Sainte-Reine (Roman Alesia) supports this view. In the cellar of a private dwelling, in a room used for the practice of domestic cults, was found the leg of an offertory table dating from the second or third century A.D. The sculpture represents a smiling young man with abundant hair, wearing a toga that is raised to reveal the lower half of his body, up to his genitals. Folded in his garment he is cradling an outstretched cat, which is wearing a bell collar around its neck.

Several examples of this kind of sculpted pedestal, which probably supported tables on which offerings of fruit were deposited, were found on the site of Alesia, in basement rooms generally given over to the worship of the Mater, protective goddess of the family. Such private underground sanctuaries seem to have been a feature of provincial Gallic culture, whereas in Rome the small chapels given over to the worship of household spirits and the *genius* were located in the atrium of the dwelling. For the Romans, these *genii* (from *generare*, to engender) represented the life principle that ensured the perpetuity of the dynasty. Did the Gauls have a similar

Young man with cat found in 1937 on the site of Roman Alesia (second or third century A.D.).

cult, or did they adopt it after the Roman conquest?

Some scholars have seen in the young man with the cat a representation of a "young Priapus" (Espérandieu), or of the Phrygian shepherd god Attis, unhappy lover of Cybele. In any case, the *genius* of Mount Auxois, ostentatiously displaying his genitals, shows clearly that he is a fertility god. As for the cat, we know that the Gauls represented animals on their statues to emphasize certain qualities: strength, agility, and so on. In this case the cat was probably chosen as a symbol of fertility, and also, perhaps, for its power to ward off evil spirits, as seems to be suggested by the bell around its neck. A Celtic statue of a seated cat, found in 1856 near Auxerre, on the site of Autessiodorum, and dating from somewhere between the first century B.C. and the second century A.D., bears a similar collar, but without a bell. Is it warding off evil spirits? Very likely, since the cat was associated with the protective household gods. It is certainly a domestic cat; its relaxed pose in the youth's arms, its tranquil air, and its collar all testify to this.

N I N E   L I V E S   O R   N I N E   T A I L S ?

Everyone knows that a cat has nine lives. At least, this is a country belief that still persists and contributes to the aura of mystery surrounding the cat. The idea that the cat can reincarnate itself makes sense to those who believe it to be a magical animal, a creature possessed of supernatural powers. It's also possible that the cat's hardy resistance to pain and illness gave rise to its reputation for having several lives. The English seem to have perpetuated this belief in the nineteenth century, in the nickname for the whip used to flog sailors: "cat-o'-nine-tails."

But the key to this belief is to be found much further back in history, in ancient Egypt. In many cosmogonies the number nine is of paramount importance. Whether it is attached to celestial spheres or infernal circles, muses or angelic hierarchies, nine, the square of three, has a ritual value. It is the number that represents the sum total, universality, achievement. Pharaonic religion was no exception to this "rule of nine."

According to the theologians of Heliopolis, Atum-Ra, the creating sun, gave birth to two couples: Shu (air) and Tefnut (moisture); and Geb (earth) and Nut (sky), his wife. These last, in turn, begat Osiris and Isis, Seth and Nephthys. As the author of a religious text from Deir el-Bahari, dating from the

Twenty-second Dynasty, proclaims: "I am one who becomes two; I am two who become four; I am four who become eight; I am one more after that." The primordial nine thus represents a unity.

A hymn from the fourth century B.C. addressed to Ra, the sun of Heliopolis, offers a key to this puzzle. It runs: "O sacred cat! Your mouth is the mouth of the god Atum, the lord of life who has saved you from all taint." Thus the cat is invested with the creative power of Atum-Ra, the unique, who is nine even as he is one. Doubtless it was for this reason that the Egyptian priests, and thenceforth popular superstition, began to credit the cat with the privilege of nine successive lives.

CRICKET ON THE HEARTH

The cat, household god and protective spirit of the family, soon gravitated to the very heart of the house, the hearth. Traditionally this was the entrance and exit for both good and bad spirits, for the sorceress as well as for Santa Claus. As we watch cats dreaming in front of the flames, we may find ourselves remembering these words of Herodotus:

When there is a fire, cats are possessed of a supernatural fury: it is in vain that the Egyptians seek to prevent them approaching it; everyone stands in a row, a little distance from his neighbor, trying to protect the cats, who nevertheless slip through the line or jump over it, and hurl themselves into the flames.

The cat has tamed fire, and it is proud of its conquest. And the peasants whose homes it shared were quick to notice this fondness for the hearth, the focus of household life. A cat new to the house was immediately taken to the hearth to ensure that it would not run away, as this sixteenth-century extract from a book of lore attests:

Anyone who wants his cat to remain in the house should take the animal and walk it three times around the milk pail, and then rub the paws against the wall of the chimney, and it is certain that the cat will never depart from that house.

This introduction to the heart of the house was completed by an offering of food — proof, if proof

Getting on like cats and dogs: fifteenth-century church stall misericord. Rodez Cathedral, France.

were needed, that our ancestors had a fine perception of cat behavior. "A woman who wants to keep her good cat should oil its four paws with butter on three successive evenings, and never shall that cat depart the house." This ceremony combined elements of paganism, superstition, and religious fear. Thus, in the region of Liège, after taking care to butter the cat's paws, the new owner walked his cat three times

whole thing caused quite a stir, and dogs and cats went to settle their differences before the tribunal of St. Peter. The verdict was recorded on a piece of parchment given to a dog historian. The cat was granted the 12 night hours by the hearth, while dogs could claim possession during the day. With characteristic cunning the cats progressively encroached on the daytime period, and in no time at all open conflict had once again broken out. Up in Heaven, St. Peter, angered by the concert of meows and barks, summoned the plaintiffs to a second hearing. Just then a mouse trotted through the audience chamber. A cat leapt on it and gobbled it up, to the great astonishment of the dog, whose mouth gaped open so that he dropped the parchment. Another tomcat gulped this down and a general brawl ensued. St. Peter, at the end of his rope, sent them all back down to earth. Since then, dogs and cats have always battled for the better place in front of the fire, a struggle one can be fairly sure will continue until the end of time.

around the milk pail and then forced it to scratch the fireplace wall with its front paws. In the Gironde the animal was required to make the sign of the cross on the chimney, just in case some demon might be lurking in the flue.

The cat, however, was obliged to defend its place at the fireside against its eternal enemy. The story of the war between cats and dogs for possession of the hearth, a distant echo of the struggles between nocturnal cults and open religion, is passed down to us in a Walloon legend. Man's best and most faithful friend, guardian of the house and the children, did not accept the cat's intrusion into his domain. The

Cat and dog fighting over a snack: fifteenth-century carved capital from the convent of the Cordeliers, Troyes, France.

THE GREEN-EYED GOD

The green glow that seems to light up a cat's eyes in the darkness, while enchanting those who have already fallen under the creature's spell, has also served further to discomfit people already made uneasy by the cat's aura of impenetrable "otherness."

The Irish Celts believed that the eye of a cat was a portal to the other world, while the Egyptians felt terror and awe toward a green-eyed cat, for the sacred texts state that when Atum-Ra created the universe by raising his voice above the primordial chaos the gestating universe was colored green.

The English poet, William Blake, perhaps had the flame-like luminescence of a night-hunting cat's eyes in mind when he wrote of its larger relative, the tiger, "Burning bright/ In the forests of the night." In fact, as anyone who drives along unlit country roads at night will know, the eyes of any nocturnal animal will stand out as pinpoints of light against the surrounding darkness if caught in a headlight's beam, and in the case of the cat it seems that it is not the glowing eyes, but their greenness that unsettles us.

Green is a color that has always had mixed associations. The English think of the greenness of their temperate, fertile landscape as a symbol of home and comfort, but when personified, in the form of the Green Man, it also symbolizes the old gods who

haunted the aboriginal forest and may still lurk, after dark, in their trim groves. Green is the color of the spring shoots and the village square, but also the color of corruption; under a green light the blood is drained from our faces and we see the fate that must befall our flesh.

Green is at one and the same time the color of growing things and of decomposition, of divinity and the devil. St. John describes the God of Revelations as "like a jasper and a sardine stone: and there was a rainbow round about the throne, in sight like unto an emerald." Emeralds are the stones of ill omen, and it was not by chance that the medieval artists chose panels of green glass for the eyes of the devil in the windows of Chartres Cathedral.

Green, this equivocal color flashing in the cat's eye, arouses passionate reactions. Was it, in fact, the cat, the furtive, thieving cat of so many people's distorted imagination that led us to personify jealousy as the green-eyed goddess whose malevolent influence causes us to "turn green with envy" when we witness another's good fortune? If so, we have gravely slandered an animal that chooses to accept our hospitality on its own terms and, unlike its canine rivals for our affections, clearly feels no envy whatsoever toward its human hosts.

B E W A R E   T H E   B L A C K   C A T

Throughout history, no animal close to man has so vividly evoked his fear of the unknown, his terror of the dark, his complicity with the devil, as — inadvertently — the black cat. More than all other domestic cats, the one with fur dark as night became, in the popular imagination, the witch's familiar, the sorcerer's apprentice. In the collective unconscious of the Middle Ages the black cat, its coat almost a caricature of the priest's robes, became a wielder of power, a carrier of bad luck, a symbol of wantonness and iniquity, catalyst of unspoken fears and unspeakable desires, Satan metamorphosed into an ambiguous ball of fur, all sparks and sulphur.

Having achieved divine status in Ancient Egypt, a living idol brought from the East, the cat arrived in Europe shrouded in mystery. Associated with the last priestesses of lunar cults, it was viewed as an alien of unknown origin whose intense and indefinable presence disturbed the newly established order of Christianity.

Pagan cults had been banned since the fourth century; in 557 A.D. the Council of Tours forbade Christians, under pain of excommunication, to make sacrifices to the dead or to indulge in any of the other rituals disapproved of by the Church. The first victims of these edicts were the wise women and folk-healers, experts in the art of curing with natural

OPPOSITE **Palma di Falco (1886–1988): model for a cat fountain. Plaster.**

remedies, who had inherited the healing functions of the earth-mother goddesses along with their symbol. Their familiar was, naturally, a black cat, a creature of earthly animal magnetism, whose very appearance provoked fear. As Moncrif, the first to rehabilitate the animal, wrote in 1727 in his *History of Cats*: "It is true that the color black works very much against cats in unsophisticated minds: it heightens the fire of their eyes, which is enough to make people believe they are witches at the very least."

By the Middle Ages the color black had already acquired disquieting associations. It had earlier been linked with renewal and fertility, notably in Egypt, until the reign of Psammetichus II (594–588 B.C.). This sovereign, wanting to stigmatize the Ethiopian usurpers who had preceded him, destroyed their statues and laid a curse on "the black Ethiopian," associating him with the evil god Seth. This fusion of black with evil was to continue into the Middle Ages, where monastic texts often liken the devil to an Ethiopian or to a "little Negro." Nor should we forget that most of the mother-goddesses of the Indo-European pantheons, from Kali through Isis to Diana, were also represented with black features. Only when these goddesses were subsumed into the cult of the Virgin Mary, from the Gothic period onward, do we find a quite pagan proliferation of black virgins in European churches.

The general panic that preceded the coming of the millennium and its anticipated catastrophes exposed the cat to the full animosity of the clergy. Two centuries later, the return of the Crusaders and the epidemics of black plague heralded the doleful period of cat massacres. In his Bull *Vox in Rama* (1233), Pope Gregory IX denounced the diabolical black cat that appeared on the German Sabbat. All Europe hunted down the animal. In 1307 the Bishop of Coventry was accused of adoring a black cat, as were the Knights Templar during their trials in the same period. All the evils of the earth were laid at the door of the black cat, who along with the goat was guest of honor at witches' Sabbats. As Jean Vartier wrote in *Animals on Trial*:

The black cat's great misfortune is to appear in people's eyes as an initiate isolated in a community of non-initiates, who, fearing it, are ready to persecute and destroy it, if allowed to act with impunity. Hence the ritual precautions surrounding the execution: selecting a date according to the apogee of the solar cycle; selecting a means of persecution which reunites all the ideal conditions of purification.

Here we find a partial explanation for the Fires of St. John's Eve, in which so many black cats perished. The only ones to escape the holocaust were those cats who had a tuft of white hair in their black coat, usually situated on the breast. This mark of innocence was called the "angel's mark" or "God's finger," and inspired the torturers to mercy; hence the relative rarity today of absolutely black cats, these massacres having operated a form of selection.

The anxiety aroused by the black cat was still evident in the nineteenth century, in the work of Edgar Allen Poe, who made it the incarnation of a murderer's tormented conscience in his famous story. In France at least the animal was rehabilitated, when Rodolphe Salis opened his literary cabaret, *Le Chat Noir*, in Montmartre in 1881. This bastion of the Parisian intelligentsia could hardly have chosen a better symbol to represent the spirit of creativity that was to surprise and scandalize the conservative bourgeoisie of the Third Republic.

This may have been some small reward to the inoffensive animal who paid dearly for the affront for which the Church convicted it—that of being a living insult to the white lamb of the Eucharist.

O L D   W I V E S '   T A L E S

A black cat crossing your path brings misfortune, especially if it comes from the left — everyone, or at least everyone who dislikes cats — knows this. What would these unfortunates say if they had the least idea of the alarming number of superstitions engendered by the cat, most of which are thankfully forgotten? These superstitions are a legacy of the rural mentality, and each country region has its own. Although the cat was tolerated on farms for its rat-catching abilities, it remained a mysterious animal inspiring little or no trust. The contrasting nocturnal habits of our two traditional household pets inspired the saying: "The dog wakes thrice to watch over his master, the cat wakes thrice to strangle him."

To meet a cat on the first day of the year was to be doomed to 365 days of bad luck, or so it was claimed in the Vosges; in Normandy, superstitious businessmen, on their way to settle a deal, would abandon the expedition if they happened to see a cat on the way. There is a saying: "Don't never cross a road what a black cat cross't, ain't nothing but sorrow, 'taint nothing but loss." In Provence, the innocent spectacle of cats playing in the morning was the harbinger of a wasted day. Every region had an hour or moment of the day when a chance encounter with a cat would bring bad luck, with the obvious consequence that the cat was then blamed for any

and all of the myriad problems that daily life offers as a matter of course. It hardly needs to be added that to meet a black cat at midnight was to encounter Satan in the flesh. Everywhere the cat was supposed to bring trouble.

To dream of a cat is generally regarded as a bad omen. Walloons mistrusted any cat who came to be petted; it was the sure sign of a coming betrayal. They were careful not to speak ill of anyone in front of a cat, for to do so was to ensure that the subject would immediately find out what was being said behind his or her back. In Brittany, people avoided confiding secrets in the presence of a cat, even if it was asleep, for fear that the secret would soon be spread abroad.

It was said that the only good cat was a stolen cat, and so people avoided buying them. In Anjou, this animal of ill omen was supposedly capable of preventing bread from rising (or of causing it to burn) if it entered a bakery when the baker was putting the dough in the oven. Certain parts of a cat's body provoked irrational fears. In Normandy, a cat's ear would be severed so that it could no longer get to the Sabbat, while in Brittany, it was thought that removing the tail prevented the cat from changing into a witch. In the west of France it was believed that the devil dwelt in the tip of a cat's tail, and it

was for this reason that it sometimes lashed so furiously. Out of prudence and a fear of poison, this "devil's hair" was cut off.

In spite of all this, a cat's death was everywhere considered to presage misfortune, especially when it took place in the home, a sure sign that one of the members of the family would shortly disappear. In Germany, two cats fighting in front of a sick person's dwelling meant that the invalid would shortly die, and the presence of a black cat on a gravestone indicated that the devil had taken possession of the soul of the departed. On the other hand, two cats seen fighting near a dying person or on the grave shortly after a funeral were said to be the devil and an angel fighting for possession of the soul. In Tuscany, people avoided reference to a deceased person for fear of seeing him appear with a cat's face. In contrast, in Sicily, no one would ever have thought of mistreating a cat, for the animal was considered sacred to St. Martha.

But the oddest superstitions of all concerned the birth of cats in the month of May. To begin with, it was thought that the tomcat himself destroyed this unlucky progeny, and if he didn't, it was wise to do it oneself, because "there's nothing worse than a cat born in May." Such cats brought snakes into the house, or would, given the chance, suffocate babies in their cradles. Until recently it was thought that kittens born in this month were dirty and untrainable. There is a Huntingdonshire proverb that attests to this, derived from the cat's link with the goddess Freya in her more licentious aspect:

May chets

Bad luck begets

And sure to make dirty cats.

Freya was an earth goddess with connections to Bast and Aphrodite. Lover, mother, and destroyer, her chariot was drawn by two cats. When the old gods were discredited, Freya's aspect as fertility goddess was transmuted into a reputation for lasciviousness. May was traditionally the month when people all over Europe refrained from sexual intercourse to purify themselves for the great midsummer celebrations held in June. Thus, as symbols of the wanton Freya, kittens born in May would have been ritually unclean and it would have been necessary to destroy them. It is still considered unlucky to marry in this month, as the sayings have it: "Marry in May, you'll rue the day," or "Wicked women get married in May." Such curious beliefs seem to be an echo of that Christian tradition that demands respect for the month of May, sacred to the Virgin Mary, during which no other marriage could be celebrated. This religious prohibition was compounded by a more pagan fear, as is underlined by Claude Gaignebet: "We were held back by fear from births that might take place nine months later, that is to say in mid-carnival, in the mid-period of madness."

T H E   G O L D E N   C A T

If you can work up the courage, go at midnight to a forest on the night of the full moon and there, where four paths meet, call up the devil. He will appear to you in the form of a black cat. A few drops of blood from your left hand at the bottom of a parchment, and buried treasure and riches unimaginable are yours. You have nothing to lose — except, of course, in the end, your immortal soul...

This was common belief in the countryside not so long ago, and it was thought that the cat, like the dragon and the magic snake, was the guardian of buried treasure. There is a Tuscan tale of a very poor village woman who, wandering in the mountains, found herself by chance in the mysterious realm of the cats. She immediately made herself useful, cleaning up, washing the dishes, and preparing a meal, whereupon the King of the Cats, before sending her home, filled her apron with pieces of gold. Back in her village, the woman told the story to her jealous sister, who also wanted to try her luck. But she treated the cats badly and returned with nothing but scratches and bites.

Cats were thought to be linked with the infernal deities and thus privy to the arcane secrets of the gold of knowledge, a sort of "cat who laid the golden egg," as shown in the story of Puss in Boots, who leads his master to riches and power. It used to be

The cat, the shortest way to riches, at least in the Middle Ages.

said of a lucky woman that "she's found the golden cat." How can you tell a gold-bringing cat from an ordinary cat? First of all by its color: black, naturally. Then by its strange behavior: lazy, not inclined to chase mice, preferring to spend its days warming itself by the hearth, eating and even dancing (sic), the magical animal played its real role only after nightfall. In some regions it was thought that the

magic would work only if the mistress of the house offered the cat her breast and suckled it. But generally it was enough to place a purse containing a golden coin next to the cat before going to bed, and whisper in its ear: "Do your duty." Come morning the purse would be filled with gold pieces, and it was customary to thank the cat with a bowl of nice thick gruel.

There was only one problem with the gold-bringing cat, whose longevity was as remarkable as its talents; it served nine masters in turn, but carried the soul of the ninth to hell, which incited its owners to get rid of it as soon as possible once they'd made their fortune. Yield wasn't always guaranteed, however, and any disappointments were invariably laid at the cat's door. In his *Veillées bretonnes* (Breton Evenings) F. M. Luzel tells how, in the nineteenth century, a man from the Belle-Isle-en-Terre region, having bought a "golden cat" from an old peasant woman for three hundred francs, demanded a refund in front of witnesses because, for eight consecutive nights, the cat had brought no return. The case caused quite a stir and was arbitrated by a Justice of the Peace. The latter obliged the old woman to hand back the purchase price, on the grounds that the cat had proved "unproductive."

C U R I O S I T Y   K I L L E D   T H E   C A T

The ritual sacrifice of cats is a European tradition that began in the Middle Ages, and continued in some places right up to the beginning of this century. The animals' horrible fates ranged from being buried or burned alive to being walled in or simply butchered. It is hard to fathom the rationale behind these ghastly holocausts, which were officially sanctioned and took place regularly all over Europe. Did those who carried them out even know why they were doing it, or were they simply superstitious, blindly reenacting the barbaric customs of their ancestors?

One widespread tradition was the enclosing of a cat, often still alive, in the foundations of a new house, castle, or public building. A number of desiccated corpses have been found during the restoration or demolition of old buildings in Britain, France, and Switzerland. You can still see one at Rouen, between two beams at the Aitre Saint-Maclou, the old charnel house where the bodies of plague victims were stored. One explanation is that this was supposed to be a way of warding off evil, or perhaps walling up a cat was intended to ensure that a building retained its *genius loci* for good.

From ancient times, the cat has been associated with water and fertility and was therefore regarded in rural communities as an appropriate sacrifice to

Cat found walled up at Rans, canton of St. Gall, Switzerland.

ensure a good harvest, replacing the human sacrifices of old. In one ritual, the cat would be garlanded with ribbons; in another, it would be impersonated by a man covered in ears of corn. In most areas, however, from Europe to the great plains of Central Asia, a cat really was sacrificed, either buried beneath the newly sown crop, or beaten to death, as a symbol of the grain that was threshed and smoothed out in order that it should grow again, returning stronger than ever in the spring.

This custom, which formed part of the Celtic *Lugnasad*, or harvest festival, probably dated from

the Neolithic period, like the traditional solstice fires whose origins are lost in the mists of time. When these customs, along with numerous pagan festivals, were revived and appropriated by the Christian religion, the burning of cats became a regular occurrence in almost every part of Europe. The Church's view was that these customs were all part of the struggle against evil, of which, of course, the cat was the incarnation. The sacrifice of cats was also thought to be a slaughter of witches, as was believed in one instance at Metz; a woman condemned to the stake having been secretly saved from burning, a black cat was substituted under cover of the dense smoke. The animal, howling and half-burnt, succeeded in escaping and disappeared into the crowd, who were convinced that they had seen the soul of the dead witch pass by.

As the old pagan festivals were absorbed into the medieval tradition, fires became a feature of many festivals, from that of St. John (the summer solstice), to All Hallow's Eve (the Celtic *Samhain*), and Christmas (the winter solstice). The flames symbolized both purification and fertility, and throughout the Middle Ages and beyond, the immolation of cats in such fires was a popular celebration that incorporated various traditions. In some cases the cat was suspended from a pole, traditionally associated with May Day, to make more of the spectacle. In Paris, cats were hung in a basket over a huge bonfire on the Place de Grève, and the King himself applied the funeral torch, watched by the entire populace, Louis XIV being the last monarch to preside over this ceremony, as late as 1648. During the coronation of

Queen Elizabeth I, a number of cats were stuffed into a wicker effigy of the Pope, the whole thing thrown on a bonfire where the screams of the cats were said to be the demons of the dying Pope. In the Belgian town of Ypres, by contrast, the cats were simply thrown from the top of the belfry. The links between these festivities and the ancient ceremony designed to alleviate the sufferings of souls in purgatory and to obtain good harvests was soon forgotten. All that was left was the general notion of purification, a need to purge the community of the forces of evil. This meant eradicating any vestiges of the forbidden cults; as a witch wasn't always available, and the devil was too elusive, it was the cats who paid the price.

The cat had happier associations in European folklore than those suggested by its ritual burning. It was, for instance, a common feature of the signs that hung above the entrances to numerous workshops in the little streets of medieval towns.

In his novel *La Maison du chat qui pelote* Balzac describes in detail a dry goods shop in the Rue Saint-Denis in Paris, where a painted canvas hanging from an old beam featured a rather eccentric cat: "The animal held in one of its front paws a racket almost as large as itself, and stood on its hind legs, gazing at a huge ball thrown by a gentleman in an embroidered outfit." They are playing the game of *pelote*.

Balzac speculates that the painter of this naive picture wanted either to "mock the merchant and passersby" or to commemorate the exploits of a highly gifted cat who had once excelled at this game. But perhaps the painter was simply making a pun, playing a pictorial word game where the image hid a meaning accessible only to initiates or observant passersby. The French *"chat qui pelote"* sounds just the same as *"chaque y pelot"*—all will find profit here. We might also infer that this Balzacian cat, playing a game that had once been the preserve of the aristocracy — and, moreover, in the company of a gentleman — acted as a discreet sign to a royalist club. And the choice of the word "*peloter*," which could also mean, in this case, to thrust and parry, whether in conversation or in combat, suggests that people lingered here making small talk while awaiting the occurrence of something more serious — a conspiracy, for example.

Such punning images were a feature of heraldry, and the cat has played its part in the symbolism. The most famous of the Roman legions, the *Felices seniores*, bore the cat on their arms, punning on the words *felis* (cat) and *felix* ("fortunate"). In the fifth century the cat was adopted as a symbol of liberty and independence by Gundiracus, King of Burgundy. And in due course the cat came to feature on more than a hundred European coats-of-arms (often with a punning meaning, like Balzac's cat — in heraldry this is called canting) such as those of the families of Lechat, Gatti, Katzen, Lecat, and Katzmair. British heraldry's most celebrated cat is on the crest of the City of Coventry, although it has probably evolved over the years from the original leopard. The crest of the Grants of Ballindalloch in Scotland features a mountain cat and the motto "Touch not gloveles," while the Macintosh clan bears the same motto beneath a crest supported by two cats. But in Britain, again, the animal tends to feature in heraldry less for its symbolic associations than for the pleasure of making a pun; many families with names vaguely resembling "cat" have adopted domestic or wild cats, or even tigers and leopards, into their coats-of-arms, among them Keat, Cattley, Catesby, and Caton.

The cat has never enjoyed the same popularity in heraldic representation as its larger relative, the lion. Nevertheless, whether crouching in fear or rampant (upright on its back legs), bristling (back raised, fur erect), or armed (with claws of a different color from the body), a cat in a coat-of-arms represents at least as much as the lion those qualities of independence and freedom for which it is famed. It was in this spirit, no doubt, that Dorothy Sayers gave her fictional detective, the insouciant Lord Peter Wimsey, a crest featuring "a domestic cat couched as to spring, proper," and the motto "As my whimsy takes me."

To the Egyptians the cat was a divine creature, born in the heart of Heaven, the site of the constellation of the Lion. This belief seems to have arisen because of the mythological origins of the goddess Bastet. Ra, the sun god, the story goes, was angered by man's rebellion against his authority and despatched to earth one of his daughters, the Eye of the Sun, who arrived in the Nubian desert in the shape of a bloodthirsty lioness, a sort of Fury. Variously identified with Hathor, Tefnut, and above all with Sekhmet ("the Powerful One"), wife of Ptah, this divine harridan revelled in a frenzy of slaughter, causing epidemics and widespread bloodshed. Then Ra sent the warrior god Enouris down to earth with orders to curb Sekhmet. Once tamed, the lioness transformed herself into a cat. Thus was born the goddess Bastet, with her volatile nature, and this is how the constellation of the Lion gave birth to the cat.

Western astronomy neglected *Felis catus*, which was not included among the thirty-three animals featured on the old sky maps. However, at the end of the eighteenth century, the French astronomer Joseph-Jérôme Lalande, in rearranging the stars into different constellations, nominated the cat for a small one which he called "Faelis." "I am very fond of cats," he wrote. "I will let this figure scratch on the chart."

The mysterious cats of the Tarot: the Menor dalla Gatta Well. Venice, fifteenth century.

The constellation was situated in the southern hemisphere, near the Hydra, and figured in an important map, the *Atlas Caelestis* of Johan Elert Bode (Berlin, 1805), but within a hundred years it was found to be redundant and was expunged from the heavens.

But in Chinese astrology, as popularized in the West, the cat does indeed have a place among the animals of the Zodiac. Even here, however, it features only as a substitute, because this fourth sign,

69

as does that of Nicolas Conver (Marseilles, 1761). In the Marseilles Tarot from the nineteenth century on, on the other hand, the cat has metamorphosed into a dog.

According to one appealing tradition, the tarot originated in Egypt. Other authorities hold that it originated in Venice, the source of the earliest known game, dating from the fourteenth century. Cats were venerated in both places, and there is nothing surprising about the presence on the card of a cat warning mankind against the powers, both good and evil, of the nocturnal world.

Some have seen the Fool as a representation of unconscious man, blind to the knowledge tied up in his beggar's bag, teetering toward the abyss. But this "madman" striding away from the city, pilgrim's staff in hand, can also be a wise man, an initiate, a master, one who feels the need to retire from the solar world, to meditate in lonely places bathed in the clear light of the moon toward which he is advancing. We know the hidden significance of the "Fools' Festivals" that flourished in the medieval period. Furthermore, the Fool, this card without a number, is as much the 0 as the 22; like the joker in a pack of playing cards, it is exempt from the rules that govern its fellows, outside the 21 cards of the major arcana, and clearly symbolizes the idea of renewal, the need for reflection at the dawning of a new era. And with his aggressive cat, vigilant guardian of the threshold, to keep him alert, this "madman" holds in his hand all the aces that will enable him to arrive safely at his journey's end.

corresponding to our Cancer, is more properly called the hare, whose lunar and nocturnal symbolism has much in common with that of the cat.

The cat does make a spectacular appearance on the last image of the tarot's major card, the Fool. This card, which is unnumbered, shows a vagabond wearing an elaborate hat, with a stick in his hand and a sack on his shoulder. His shoes are torn, and a white and red cat is biting his leg. This animal has come and gone over the centuries. The Visconti Tarot (Milan, *c.* 1430) omits it altogether, while the earliest version of the Marseilles Tarot (*c.* 1700) includes it,

THE ALCHEMICAL CAT

The cat was admitted into the secret of the alchemist's cabinet, as is evident from the engraving on the flyleaf of Lambsprinck's treatise, *De Lapide Philosophico* (The Philosopher's Stone, 1677). This depicts a majestic white cat emerging from a cave, inside which a dragon lurks, and above which we see the sun god Jupiter.

Both male and female, creature of sun and shade, moon and water, the cat, once venerated in Egypt, came to represent for devotees of the occult a model of hermetic androgyny. The writer Fulcanelli (1877–1932) suggests this in *The Mystery of the Cathedrals*:

...and if you know why the Egyptians deified the cat, there will no longer be any room for doubt about the subject you must choose; its common name will be clearly known to you. You will then be in possession of this Chaos of Sages, which contains all the hidden secrets.

Mythology has made the cat a repository of secrets, because the X shape of its whiskers represents the Greek letter *khi*, the initial letter of *chaos* (the alchemist's *prima materia*), and also of the Greek words for crucible, gold, and time — the triple unknown of the Grand Design. Thus the X formed by the cat's whiskers represents "light formed by light." When Fulcanelli's disciple Eugène Canseliet was studying the occult symbolism of the bench ends of the choir stalls in the Cathedral of St. Pierre at

Poitiers, he saw the image of a cat pouncing on a rat as a metaphor for the solar fire consuming sulphur.

The variations in the color of the cat's coat can also be interpreted as symbolic of different phases of the Design. When it is black, it suggests raw material; when russet (as in Jean Stradano's painting in the alchemical laboratory of Francisco I de' Medici, in Florence), it symbolizes secret fire.

During the trial of the Knights Templar in 1307, various members of the order who had been accused of worshipping a statuette named Baphomet described it either as a bearded demon (reminiscent of the Egyptian god Bes) with four legs, or else as a gray or black cat. Bernard de Salgues testified that this cat spoke to him at Montpellier, while Jean de Nériton confessed that the feline idol gave promises of abundant harvests, gold, and good health. On the face of it, one might conclude that the cat was being used as a scapegoat; it is worth remembering, however, that the accusation against the Templars was that they had tried to bring about a *rapprochement*, through this Baphomet, with the Islamic world — which, let us not forget, was where the domestic cat had come from. In several interpretations, Baphomet has many parallels with Mohammed. Was his worship a fusion of Christianity and Islam, or were the adherents of Baphomet reviving the mystical heresy of the Gnostics, as is suggested by those theories on the etymology of the name that maintain that it comes from *baphe meteos* (baptism of fire) or *Ouba-el-Phoumet* (the Mouth of the Father)? Others translate Baphomet as "dyer of the moon," which for alchemists was another way of saying "he who holds

the key to the Grand Design." The rare images of Baphomet present a real alchemical puzzle: a bearded winged demon, with horns and claws, female breasts, and erect penis, symbol of the fulfillment of the Design.

This manifestation of the androgynous feline of Egypt makes a prominent appearance at the apex of the façade of the church of St. Merri des Halles in Paris, a few steps from the house of Nicolas Flamel, most famous of medieval alchemists. Why give the demon the position normally reserved for Christ? It seems that this was done in 1842, when the church was restored by the followers of the architect and archaeologist Viollet-le-Duc, to draw attention to the presence of such a strange discovery in such a place. The statue may originally have featured less prominently among those in the niches of the façade. It is thought that Baphomet was also depicted by the door of the south transept of Notre Dame in Paris, that great open book of alchemy.

The enigmatic Baphomet. Église
St. Merri, Paris.

72

THE ECCLESIASTICAL CAT

Although the Church, in the person of Pope Gregory IX and subsequent accusers, set itself firmly against the cat throughout the Middle Ages, it would be wrong to assume that every priest, monk, and nun reacted in the same way. There is a considerable body of evidence, from illustrated manuscripts, miniatures, and church carvings, testifying to the presence of cats. Fear, incomprehension, even accusations of diabolism, could not inhibit Christians' overtures toward a useful domestic animal that was also good company.

This secret alliance appears to have been first sealed in the British Isles, and especially in Ireland. By 700 A.D. the cat was already appearing in the illuminations of the Lindisfarne Gospels, and there are numerous cat illustrations in the *Book of Kells*, produced *c.* 800 A.D. by artists working in an Irish monastery. At the foot of the tenth-century Celtic cross of Muireadach in Monasterboice, a pair of recumbent cats can be seen holding between their paws a fledgling bird and a kitten (or is it a mouse?) and a cat features in the carvings on the portal of the church at Clonfert. It is tempting to wonder if St. Columba, the founder of Western monasticism, who left Ireland to set up new communities in Europe, may have had a determining influence in favor of the cat. An Irish poem, written by a monk in the eighth

or ninth century (and set to music by Samuel Barber in 1953), extols the charms of the cloistered life with a cat as sole companion:

> *Pangur, white Pangur,*
> *How happy we are*
> *Alone together,*
> *Scholar and cat.*

The Ashmolean and Harleian bestiaries of the twelfth and thirteenth centuries, although sparing with verbal descriptions, contain numerous pictures of cats, as do English Gothic psalters such as the *Luttrell Psalter* (c. 1330) and *Queen Mary's Psalter* (early fourteenth century). During the same period, the French illustrator Jean Pucelle depicted a tomcat and an old man warming themselves at a fireplace, while servants stoke the fire with wood (*Psautier et Livre de Prières de Bonne de Luxembourg*, c. 1345), and a cat playing with a ball of yarn while a woman spins (*Livre d'Heures de Jeanne d'Evreux*, c. 1325).

Even the monastic rules prohibiting luxury refer to cats. The only furs permitted, for example, were the skins of sheep, rabbits, and cats. The cats in question would almost certainly have been wildcats, although we know that as early as the sixteenth century furriers were making great claims for the pelts

of "Chartreux cats." In spite of the name these were not cats raised by Carthusian monks (whose first monastery was La Grande Chartreuse); the reference is probably to the similarity of cats' fur to a type of Spanish wool known as *pile des chartreux*.

There are several written references to domestic cats in monasteries. A hagiography of Gregory the Great tells of a hermit living on intimate terms with a *cohabitrix* — a female cat. Edmer, a twelfth-century monk of Canterbury, describes the pleasure of stroking a white cat, and during the same period St. Hildegarde of Bingen also refers to cats. These confessions of amicable relations with cats often attracted rebukes from authority and accusations of collusion with the devil or at the very least of a tendency toward immorality. But even the Church could not entirely stamp out a regard for cats.

It is generally supposed that the Romanesque bestiary overlooked the cat, but it is tempting to suggest that inside many a lion depicted by Romanesque sculptors there is a cat trying to get out! Sometimes the matter is almost beyond doubt. A good example is the doorway of the church of Ecoman, near Châteaudun in northern France, where two cats' heads are clearly visible; at the churches of Marestay and Bagnizeau, also in France, in the south apse and the doorway respectively, there are friezes of cats' heads; and near Albi in Provence there is a similar frieze over the porch vaulting of the church of St. Michel de Lescure.

The presence of cats in this masterpiece of Benedictine Romanesque art, dating from *c.* 1150, calls for an explanation. In the iconography of the

porch of St. Michel, Hervé Rougier has correctly identified a kind of cosmic calendar. Three *khi-rho* monograms represent the summer solstice and the two equinoxes, fifty-two balls, the weeks in the year, and four arches, the seasons. Suns and moons alternate above a frieze of plant and animal motifs, out of which project twenty-three cats' heads, arranged in a semicircle. The keystone shows a larger head. If we assume that the cat, a solar and lunar symbol, was chosen to represent the twenty-four hours of day and night, it makes sense that the two eleven-hour periods come together to share in a twelfth hour that is both midday and midnight. Thus the final tally is twenty-four cats representing twenty-four hours.

The same porch contains a further twenty recumbent felines, each with two bodies and a single head. It is unclear whether they are lions or cats, but, if the latter, perhaps we have here a symbolic reminder of the cat's equivocal nature: day and night, masculine and feminine, divine and diabolical, always dual and yet at the same time unique. On the other hand, even inside some sanctuaries one comes across feline images that are more like cats than either lions or leopards, but this may well be because the sculptors in question had ready access to pet cats as their models, their knowledge of the cat's wilder cousins

being secondhand, based on travelers' tales or inaccurate drawings. The symbolism of some of the animals in the Romanesque bestiary remains equivocal. Were the various feline heads on gargoyles, for example, designed to ward off devils by the act of invoking or representing them?

Oddly enough, it was in the same period as the Papal bull *Vox in Rama* (1233), which launched so many cat massacres, that the animal's image was proliferating in Catholic sanctuaries thanks to the carvers of misericords in choir stalls. As it was forbidden to depict sacred subjects or figures in the decoration of these ledges, which enabled priests and monks discreetly to rest their backsides without appearing to sit (hence the name "misericord" or "compassion"), the carvers tended to use subjects drawn either from the wildly fantastic or from daily life, and animals played an important part. More than 270 representations of animals have been catalogued in Great Britain, France, Switzerland, Belgium, Germany, and Spain. While dogs head the list, with 26 carvings, the cat has a good second place, with 15, dating from the thirteenth to the sixteenth century: an astonishing number, given the period and the almost total silence surrounding the cat in the texts of Gothic bestiaries.

Even more surprising is the manner in which the carvers treated the subject. While the cat was being officially outlawed for its diabolical connections, not one single misericord shows the animal in an unfavorable light. Instead, the artist's chisel presents

Apse window, c. 1150. Église St. Pierre,

Marestay (Charente-Maritime), France.

familiar images: kittens in a basket, a cat washing itself, a cat lying in wait for and pouncing on mice, a cat perched on a pair of bellows by the fireside, or fraternizing with a dog. There is only one exception to the otherwise positive series of images, and that is in the fifteenth-century church of St. Sulpice at Diest in Belgium, where a farmer is shown preparing to throw a cat from his shoulders, an image that recalls the cat burnings of Ypres.

The cat also infiltrated the church via literature, with numerous scenes from the tale of *Reynard the Fox* illustrated on carved panels. Notable examples include three from Bristol Cathedral: Tybert the cat preaching (at St. Claude, in the Jura), and holding out a missal to Bernard, and the donkey archpriest (in Strasbourg Cathedral).

Should we look on the presence of these cats, and of other subjects deemed to be improper — especially scatological ones — as deliberate provocation on the part of the artists? This seems unlikely, given that the clerics who paid for the work had to agree to the subjects, very often suggesting the themes themselves. It is worth remembering, however, that although cats do sometimes appear in prominent positions, they are generally confined to the misericords in the choir stalls of cathedrals and monasteries, where they would have been concealed by a wall or rood screen from the gaze of the congregation. In other words, they were destined to be seen only by the elite. So one would imagine, at least on finding, among the grotesques depicted in the choir of the church of St. Dyé-sur-Loire, a woman with a cat's head and a lizard's tail, wearing a veil that doesn't quite cover

her feline ears. These grotesques date from the sixteenth century, and Jean Chavigny, who has made a detailed study of the village, confirms that they represent various episodes in the life of the saint known as Dyé or Deodat. He was a fifth-century hermit who fought to stop pagan rites in honor of a water god, which were being performed in a cave guarded by a dragon. It is no surprise that this reptile should be depicted in church with the face of a feline mother-goddess; it represents a return to first principles, and the artist has merely rendered unto Caesar that which is Caesar's. However, there is surely something ironic and provocative about choosing to place this extraordinary figure so close to the tabernacle.

THE MYSTERY OF THE "RAT GLOBES"

Of all the subjects tackled by sculptors in the Gothic period, there is one that never fails to excite curiosity. It consists of a globe surmounted by a cross, riddled with holes that have clearly been gnawed by the numerous rats that can be seen crawling in and out of them. These sculptures and carvings, of which few exist, are known as "rat globes," and the most famous example can be seen on the Jews' Door of the Cathedral of St. Siffrein in Carpentras, Provence. Dating from the fifteenth century, it is carved in relief and has given rise to a variety of interpretations. Some have seen it as an anti-Semitic symbol: Jews devouring Christianity (the Jews' Door was the entrance used by new converts making their way to the baptismal fonts). But this overtly offensive interpretation is not supported by other examples of rat globes — in the crypt of St. Sernin in Toulouse, at the foot of a gargoyle at St. Germain l'Auxerrois in Paris, above a buttress at Le Mans Cathedral, and on misericords in a number of churches — which have no particularly anti-Semitic connotations. So what does it mean? Although, in the Gothic bestiary, rats were sometimes used to represent Jewry, they also symbolize greed. The most likely explanation is that sculptors and craftsmen intended this enigmatic imagery to represent the sins and heresies gnawing at the Christian world. Given that all the rat globes date from the fifteenth and sixteenth centuries, it is possible, as Jean-Louis Vaudoyer maintains, that the heresy in question is the Reformation.

The sculptors who worked in churches and cathedrals were always ready to illustrate maxims or create visual puns. Perhaps the rats devouring the world

"Rat globe": sixteenth-century misericord. Église St. Anne, Gassicourt (Yvelines), France.

represented a warning to suppress those earthly appetites that destroy the soul. Others have seen it as a pagan motif, a coded rallying point for gypsies on the road from Chartres to Les Saintes Maries de la Mer. However, the most complete example of a rat globe (and now, alas, because of pollution, the least decipherable), that of St. Germain l'Auxerrois, includes an additional figure—that of a cat, lying in wait for the devouring rats. One interpretation is "that the robbers who are devouring the earth are about to be devoured by the devil." This hypothesis, however, seems to overlook the fact that the rats were themselves a symbol of the devil. Can evil be exterminated by evil?

The image of a cat stalking or eating a rat was fairly widespread in Gothic sculpture from the thirteenth century onward, and its treatment clearly demonstrates that *Felis catus* was regarded as a friendly and useful animal, skilled in destroying rodents. In the fourteenth century the Black Death claimed millions of lives all over Europe, and fear of the plague lived on in the public consciousness. It was at this time that the rat globes began to proliferate, which leads one to conclude that their role was to ward off evil, or that representing the hated animal somehow served to keep danger at bay. Thus, there is nothing diabolical about the cat's presence; quite the contrary, its role here is one of protector.

F A I T H   H E A L E R   O R   P H Y S I C I A N ?

The priests of Bastet were well versed in the two arts that are so often inextricably linked — magic and medicine. They had a range of charms, amulets, and incantations at their disposal for the treatment of mothers and their newborn babies, and used to inject children with a few drops of cat's blood to immunize them against epidemics. Long before the spread of the cult of the goddess of Bubastis, the cat was associated with Egyptian magic, as is attested by ivories and wands bearing the unmistakeable silhouette of the "Great Cat," the emanation of Atum-Ra, sometimes armed with his knife, sometimes accompanied by other benevolent creatures — lions, monkeys, etc. — or by protective spirits. This was probably "white" or defensive magic, to which the cat, invested as it was with the divine power of the sun, could clearly contribute considerable strength.

Egyptian magical token.
Steatite. Middle Kingdom.

Linked to Bastet in Egypt, then to Artemis in Greece and Diana in the Roman world, the cat remained the chosen companion of priestesses, soothsayers, and other prophetesses who, in the Middle Ages, were all classed as witches. A witch would be compelled, often under torture, to reveal the identity of her "familiar," who more often than not was a cat, or rather a demon in feline disguise. Stories abounded of terrifying metamorphoses. In Strasbourg, and at the old château of Vernon, for example, female cats were said to have attacked some upright citizens, who managed to injure some of the savage animals; the next day, several women bore traces of the wounds. Many such indictments were to lead cat and woman alike to the stake.

Why this relentless hostility to witches — and their cats? The main reason was the Church's deter-

mination to annihilate everything connected with the pagan fertility rites known as sabbats. In rural areas, women in particular would go to the wise woman rather than the priest, for she knew the art of healing with medicinal herbs, and how to deal with intimate problems of pregnancy (or, perhaps, its termination) and didn't bring morality into it. The medical profession, in its anxiety to regain its clientele, sided with the clergy. The cat had the great misfortune to be the closest companion of these old women, who, although venerated in ancient times, could not be tolerated in the Christian West because they represented a return to the bad old ways, or at least were a reminder of pagan days.

Western medicine has long considered the cat a danger to health. In *The History of Four-Footed Beasts* (1607), Edward Topsell writes:

It is most certain that the breath and savour of cats consume the radical humour and destroy the lungs, and they who keep cats with them in their beds have the air corrupted and fall into hectics and consumptions... The hair of the cat being eaten unawares stops the artery and causes suffocation.

This opinion was echoed by Ambroise Paré, the French surgeon who described the cat as "a venomous animal which infects through its hair, its breath and its brains"; while Matthiole emphasized the noxious breath that "infects with a powerful poison which causes consumption," and refers to people "who always sleep with a cat and thus become consumptive and emaciated and eventually die."

Regarding the medically beneficial properties of a cat, the 1763 edition of the *Encyclopédie* of Diderot and d'Alembert adopts a prudent position, to say the least:

Most medical writers report diverse qualities which many doctors have accorded to the various parts of the domestic cat as well as to his wild cousin... But as not one of these writers has confirmed these virtues by his own experience, we cannot count on the kind of tradition which has transmitted these claims from book to book: at the very least, before preferring these particular remedies to any others, we must wait for their virtues to be confirmed by observation.

That's all very well and possibly true, but it neglects the fact that the real healing power of the cat stems quite simply from its presence, as doctors and scientists are only now rediscovering. The cat works wonders in pediatric, psychiatric, and geriatric cases alike. The simple action of stroking a cat is wonderfully effective in reducing tension. "The nurse's favourite animal," as Champfleury called it, teaches children to be sociable, aids depressives, fills the void in the lives of the lonely, and restores old people's interest in life. This is the true therapeutic role of the cat — a gentle healing based on stroking and purring, as attested by the Reverend J.G. Wood's tribute to the nursing capabilities of his cat Prettina (1897):

The never-failing accuracy of this wise little Cat was the more surprising, because she was equally infallible by day or night. There was no striking clock in the house, so she could not have been assisted by its aid; nor was it habit, for her assiduous attentions only began with the illness, and ceased with the recovery of the invalid. Instinct, popularly so called, will not account for this wonderful capability so suddenly coming into being, and so suddenly ceasing. Surely some spirit-guiding power must have animated this sympathetic little creature, and have directed her in her labour of love.

C H I L D R E N ' S   S T O R I E S

Before its rehabilitation, which only really began in the eighteenth century, the cat enjoyed a clandestine life in literature. It is no accident that, at a time when religion and superstition had blackened its reputation, the animal tiptoed into favor through the side door of fairy tales. It is children, after all, who alter our perceptions, and the works of Perrault, Mme. d'Aulnoy, and others did more than entertain—they changed people's attitude to cats.

The theme taken up by Charles Perrault in *Le Chat Botté* (*Puss in Boots*), which appeared among the *Mother Goose Stories* (1697), was already well known, thanks largely to a story by Giovanni Straparola, which appeared in 1550. We find its echo in the English tale of Dick Whittington, which was already in circulation in the fourteenth century. This Richard Whittington, nicknamed Lord Cat, three times Lord Mayor of London between 1397 and 1417, really existed. In the story, a young country boy comes to the big city to seek his fortune, gets a job on a ship, and has the bright idea of taking his cat to sea with him. Reaching a distant country where the cat was unknown but rats, unfortunately, all too familiar, the boy makes a fortune by hiring out his companion. The grateful king showers him with gold, and he returns in triumph to London, where he receives the highest honors.

*OPPOSITE **Every white cat is a sleeping princess.***

Although Dick Whittington's cat is now commemorated by a statue on Highgate Hill, he is most definitely a creature of legend. Some commentators see his presence in the story as an interpolation of a primitive version of *Puss in Boots*. Others think that the word "cat," as used in the original story, meant a type of barge that transported coal from Newcastle to London, and not a pussycat at all. Nevertheless, this particularly positive image of the cat as a useful, affectionate, luck-bringing animal, is extremely interesting in the context of the period. The story of *Dick*

Puss in Boots: Monument to Charles Perrault. Jardin des Tuileries, Paris.

Whittington is among the most popular fairy tales of Great Britain. Offenbach composed a "fairy opera" on the theme at the request of a British impresario, and it is performed year in, year out, as a Christmas presentation.

The main difference between this and Charles Perrault's version is that the latter is a story of utter amorality, in which a cat lies, steals, schemes, and kills for the sake of a young millhand. In fact, it is an initiation story based on sources in the *Cabala*, and provides an illustration of alchemy in action.

In this tale, the youngest of the miller's three sons inherits a talking cat who demands boots, so that he can pass himself off as the servant of the Marquis of Carabas. The obvious absurdity of the story makes it clear that this is no ordinary cat, and as the story unfolds, its various elements suggest a connection with lunar magic. The cat lures a rabbit (the novice) into a bag, leads the king into temptation by offering him partridges (birds regarded as diabolic in medieval times), dunks his protégé in the river (the purifying bath), and steals the royal clothes for him, which reveal the young man's mercurial nature to the king's daughter (the virgin). Moreover, the principles of the sun and the moon can only be united by destroying the ogre, who is the incarnation of the dark forces that, in the absence of a controlling intelligence, are blindly destructive. The cat clearly shows this when he challenges the ogre to demonstrate his magical powers by turning himself into a lion and then into a mouse — which the ogre obligingly does, with obvious results. Thus, the story ends with a celebration of the alchemical marriage, in

Beauty and the Beast (Jean Cocteau, 1945): Jean Marais in cat makeup as the Beast.

which the cult of the moon is seen to regain its former place alongside the religion of the sun.

The plot of Mme. d'Aulnoy's *La Chatte Blanche*, or *The White Cat*, is not dissimilar. The youngest of a king's three sons is walking in the forest when he comes across a castle belonging to a mysterious white cat whose face is hidden under a black veil. We learn that she was once a queen, so presumably she is a lunar sovereign mourning her lost kingdom — perhaps a poetic manifestation of Diana, the hunting goddess of the crescent moon?

The white cat puts the king's son to the test, finally demanding proof of his absolute faith. He is to

cious nature and an irresistible impulse to tenderness? Three centuries after Perrault, Cocteau's film, remarkably similar to *La Chatte Blanche* in its austere, refined elegance, proves that the magic words "Once upon a time" have lost none of their hold on our imagination.

Like the Cheshire Cat, perched on his branch...

sacrifice her by cutting off her head. When he does this, the spell is broken and the cat is transformed into a golden-haired girl — the moon giving place to the rising sun. "Here is the one beyond compare," declares the old king, "the one who is worthy of my kingdom." And he bows down before the goddess, whose rightful position has now been restored.

In a similar way, through stories such as these, the cat itself regained the status it had once enjoyed before the upheavals of the Middle Ages.

In 1945 Jean Cocteau brought *Beauty and the Beast* to the screen. This famous film, *La Belle et la Bête*, is based on a story by Mme. Leprince de Beaumont. In the book the description of the Beast is fairly perfunctory, but Cocteau deliberately set out to give him a feline look. The famous mask constructed by designer Agop Arakelian for Jean Marais, who played the Beast, was apparently inspired by the features of a Persian Blue cat, Karoun. What better animal than a cat to show the conflict between a fero-

G I V E   A   C A T   A   B A D   N A M E . . .

Killing with words, when there is nothing else at hand, has always been the way of the persecutor, and the cat has certainly not escaped. Some may find this language extreme — after all, we are only talking about cats. But in the light of the violence perpetrated against cats in the course of history, it is not inappropriate to use extreme language, and to examine how the animal has been maligned.

The naturalist Buffon is rightly regarded as an enlightened thinker. Yet, when he published Volume XI of his *Histoire Naturelle* (Encyclopedia of Natural History), which dealt with cats, he was unable to conceal his aversion to the animal. The book begins with this sentence, which has become a classic of ailurophobic literature: "The cat is an unfaithful servant whom we only keep out of necessity, to combat another even more disagreeable household enemy, and one whom we cannot get rid of."

There follows a portrait of the cat in which Buffon castigates the animal for its "oblique movements," its "equivocal eyes," its sexual greed, its taste for perfumes (sic), its criminal bearing, its dishonesty, dissimulation and deceit, and the pleasure it takes in killing.

Quite apart from the animosity toward the cat as an untrustworthy "servant," there seems to be an even

more cowardly in climates which are too hot...

This could hardly be clearer, and the cat seems to have been the scapegoat for a race that people in the West chose only to know through rumor and prejudice. The accursed creature is not only the prophet Mohammed's favorite animal; it makes an unholy racket when it is excited, it steals food, as the Orientals were supposed to do, and it breeds incessantly. There is a clear parallel between Buffon's text and a racist diatribe, reinforced by numerous derogatory details. Writing at the peak of the Age of Enlightenment, Buffon is hardly a paragon of openmindedness.

As an antidote to these rancorous sentiments, it is pleasant to turn to those of François-Augustin Paradis de Moncrif, a neglected writer whose work, although uneven, is not without interest. In his *Histoire des Chats* (History of Cats, 1727), Moncrif went so far as to take up the defense of the black cat, the object of so much fear and loathing, and he suggests to its detractors that they should not be alarmed by a color that is so different from that of their own skin; for, he writes:

... in compensation, this very appearance, together with their charming ways, is for sensible people a naïve image of those African races whose dark complexion gave them a wild look, but who, once they were masters of Spain, seemed to have made the conquest of that country solely to import and establish there chivalry and courtesy.

more virulent hatred lurking behind this description. One critic has detected here an expression of all the prejudices accumulated since the Middle Ages, not only against the cat, but also, through it, against the countries from which it came. And of course it came to us from the Middle East. Even its name is derived from the Berber, Nubian, Syrian, and Arab tongues. But was Buffon a racist? This sentence from the *Histoire Naturelle* shows that the cat was not the only denizen of the Islamic world to incur his displeasure: *The different races of these animals vary in different climates in much the same way as the human races... like men, they are bigger, stronger and braver in cold countries, gentler and more civilized in moderate climates, and weaker, uglier and*

If cats have had their detractors, they have also had their defenders, one might almost say patrons, for a great many held high office, sometimes the very highest. The powerful Lord Chancellor of England, Cardinal Wolsey (1471–1530), indulged his cat in every way, including it in official audiences, admitting it to the cathedral and to all his meals. At a time when cats were being burned all over Europe, there were many who found this outrageous: "Certainly nothing like it has been seen since Caligula," sniffed the Venetian ambassador (referring to the horse Incitatus, created a Senator by the Roman Emperor).

Wolsey's pride led to his downfall, but another Prince of the Church, France's Cardinal Richelieu, had a passion for cats, and took enormous pleasure in them, always being surrounded by a dozen, which he named himself ("Lucifer," "Gazette," "Soumise," "Racan," and "Perruque," the latter two so named because they were born in the wig of Racan, the academician. He built them a cattery, employing two servants to feed them morning and evening with pâtés, and left them a generous pension in his will. But he was so hated that this provision was ignored and after his death the pensioners were massacred by the Swiss Guards.

Nineteenth-century clerics were openly enthusi-

*OPPOSITE **Palma de Falco: Two cats.***

astic about cats. Pope Leo XII (1823–29) reared one on his ermine robe, bequeathing it to the French diplomat Viscount de Chateaubriand, who recorded: *He is called Micette, and surnamed "the Pope's cat," enjoying in that regard much consideration from pious souls. I endeavor to soften his exile, and help him to forget the Sistine Chapel, and the vast dome of Saint Peter's where, far from earth, he was wont to take his daily promenade.*

The pet of Pope Pius IX (1846–78) sat on a chair opposite him at dinner, patiently waiting to be served by the Pontiff, although those of the Archbishop of Taranto ("Desdemona," "Othello," and others) ate with all the company. When the Bishop requested that one of the chaplains help the Signora Desdemona, the butler stepped forward and observed: "My lord, la Signora Desdemona will prefer waiting for the roasts," which she did, records Lady Morgan, "as well-behaved as the most *bon-ton* table in London could require."

These cat-loving clerics recall that Irish monk who enjoyed a working companionship with his white cat, Pangur Ban: "Tis a merry thing to see/ At our tasks how glad are we,/ When at home we sit and find/ Entertainment to our mind." This sentiment was echoed in a more secular age by Christopher Smart (1722–1771), who saw his cat Jeoffrey as a fellow-toiler worthy of commendation: "For he is the servant

of the living God, duly and daily serving him," and praises the way in which Jeoffrey goes briskly about his business, always behaving in a thoroughly decent English way:

For when he takes his prey he plays with it to give it a chance.
For one mouse in seven escapes by his dallying....
For the English cats are the best in Europe.

Around the same period, other cats were enjoying a more pampered life. Samuel Johnson's Hodge, clearly an arrogant fellow, was fed oysters from his master's hand, and allowed to clamber all over his ample waistcoat. Although the good doctor admitted to having had cats that he had liked better, seeing

Hodge looking out of sorts, he was quick to add: "Nevertheless Hodge is a very fine cat, a very fine cat indeed." Horace Walpole (1717–97) surrounded himself with pampered beauties, one of which, unfortunately drowned in a goldfish bowl, was immortalized in Thomas Gray's "Ode on *feue* Mademoiselle Selime," an elegant satire on Augustan verse:

The hapless nymph with wonder saw;
A whisker first and then a claw
With many an ardent wish
She stretched, in vain, to reach the prize.
What female heart can gold despise,
What cat's averse to fish?

It was in the nineteenth century, however, that cat fans really revealed themselves. Walter Scott was devoted to "Hinse of Hinsfeldt," named after the hero of a German fairy tale, but, alas, described as "venerable, fat and sleek, and no longer very locomotive." During the last year of his life, Scott visited the Bishop of Taranto mentioned above, and greatly admired the archiepiscopal felines. It was Queen Victoria, that paradigm of domestic values, who confirmed the cat as a family pet, with "White Heather" reigning supreme at Balmoral and Buckingham Palace. Cats became a feature of Victorian parlors, a symbol of the solid Victorian household. As Mark Twain wrote: "A home without a cat, and a well-fed, well petted and properly revered cat, may be a perfect home, *perhaps*, but how can it prove its title?"

But the most famous Victorian cat is probably that elusive, enigmatic creation of Lewis Carroll, the mad and logical Cheshire Cat from *Alice's Adventures in Wonderland*: "... a dog growls when it's angry, and

"From hence, ye Beauties, undeceived, Know one false step is ne'er retrieved, And be with caution bold."
(Thomas Gray, "Ode on feue Mademoiselle Selime").
Mirror handle (acacia wood) and kohl pot (enameled soapstone). Egypt, New Kingdom.

wags its tail when it's pleased. Now I growl when I'm pleased, and wag my tail when I'm angry. Therefore I'm mad."

"There are no ordinary cats," wrote Colette, and she understood them thoroughly, being surrounded with them all her life (even once appearing scandalously in a French music hall as *La Chatte Amoureuse* (The Lovesick Cat)). "I am indebted to them... for a great control over myself, for a characteristic aversion to brutal sounds and for the need to keep silent for long periods of time..." Perhaps these are the most cogent reasons for the affinity between cats and writers; another French author, Paul Léautaud, owned

over three hundred in the course of his long life, although he may simply have been overcome by the tendency described by Cocteau: "I am not one of their maniacs. I have had one, as a matter of chance, then two, four, five, and it is quite possible that, from incest to incest and birth to birth, this little troupe will become a cortège..."

Statesmen and soldiers were no more immune, although those who took a dislike to cats did so violently. Julius Caesar and Napoleon detested them (and look what became of *them*). Lenin and Winston Churchill were both cat lovers, Churchill following Wolsey and the Bishop of Taranto in reserving a place at the dining table and a seat in the Cabinet Room for Nero, who joined him at Number 10 during the war. Nero's war effort defended him against the civil servants: "He acts as a hot water bottle and saves fuel, power, and energy." The most famous Downing Street cat was an official civil servant, Wilberforce, who served from 1973 until 1986, retiring with a pension under Margaret Thatcher.

There is no cat currently at Number 10, but the position is filled at the White House, although Socks Clinton is not the first incumbent, Abraham Lincoln and Theodore Roosevelt being notable cat lovers. Like other cats in high office, Roosevelt's Slippers sat in on White House dinners and state occasions. It is not recorded whether Socks has attended any, although he has his own fan club. But happily there is yet again a first cat in America, thus proving that when it comes to pets, the cat is top dog. Which is what many people have known all along.

CATS AND THE WEATHER

People have always used animal behavior to help them to predict the weather. In the case of cats, the range of indicators is limited, although the idea, for example, that a cat with its paw behind its ear is a portent of rain to come is remarkably well established in Britain, France, Italy, German-speaking Switzerland, and elsewhere. As early as the fifteenth century, a folklorist asserted that "if you see a cat sitting in a sunny window, licking its behind and putting its paw over its ear, you can be sure of rain before the day is out," and in the seventeenth century the poet Robert Herrick referred to:

True Calendars, as Pusses eare
Washt o're, to tell what change near.

A whole body of weather lore has grown up around the various postures of cats, often owing as much to the imagination as to the observation of behavior. A cat that purrs and rubs its nose, for example, is supposed to be a sign of good weather. When it runs around and scratches the ground, storms are said to be brewing. A nervous cat presages wind, while a yawning cat is another sign of rain. If your cat goes right up to the fireplace, bad weather is on the way, and if it turns around to toast its back-side, you can expect snow.

Curiously enough, folk wisdom seems to have taken no account of the correlation between the

posture of a recumbent cat and the temperature. For the hotter the weather, the less the animal will curl up, tending instead to stretch itself out full length in order to take advantage of the coolness of the ground on which it is lying.

The association of cats with rain is not confined to Western lore. An old Cambodian custom was to take a caged cat from village to village, where the peasants would sprinkle it with water in order to persuade Indra, the beneficent Vedic deity, to send them the rainfall they needed for a good harvest.

The meteorological sensitivity of cats has been enshrined in many popular sayings. For example:

"When a cat washes its face
The weather's about to break."

Or:

"If a cat puts its paw against its ear
There's no hope of fine weather."

Such folk wisdom was codified in a song that lists all the attitudes of a cat, along with the weather conditions they were supposed to foretell.

Japanese sailors went so far as to put to sea accompanied by particolor cats known as *mike neko*, whose subtle changes of behavior gave sufficiently early warning of storms to enable the boats to get back to port in time to avoid them.

There is no doubt that cats do sense the approach of storms, earthquakes, cyclones, and volcanic eruptions, but there is nothing supernatural about it. Increased charges of static electricity and sudden variations of barometric pressure must have a lot to do with it, and an animal that spends much of its time sleeping on the floor or ground may well detect

tremors in the earth that are imperceptible to us.

What is surprising is that no one seems to have noticed that, regardless of the weather, a cat will always put its paw behind its ear when washing. The fact that a cat either is or is not fastidious about its own hygiene has very little to do with the weather!

Nevertheless, these old sayings have great charm, and none more so than the expression used by peasants in the Vosges to describe the action of a cat putting its paw behind its ear. In one of the more striking statements of belief in the power that has made the cat the farmer's ally, they say that the cat is "pulling down the rain."

A N   E A R   F O R   M U S I C

How could an animal that has sixty different sounds at its disposal with which to express itself be indifferent to music? For that matter, what music critic would have the nerve to stop a singer in mid-performance, as did the cat of Henri Sauguet, shutting a prima donna's mouth with one stroke of the paw because her voice was too shrill?

The cat has been associated with music for many centuries, thanks to the subtlety of its ear, initially in ancient Egypt, in the guise of Bastet, the goddess with the sistrum. In his treatise on Isis and Osiris, Plutarch tells us that the Egyptians regarded music as a remedy for the greatest ills; the very action of playing the sistrum shook men out of their torpor and kept at bay Seth-Typhon, "the main agent of corruption who impedes and halts the course of nature."

The sistrum is a rudimentary instrument, consisting of a handle, a shaft decorated with the faces of Isis and Nephthys, and, supported by the double head of the divine sisters, a circular frame across which are fixed four metallic rods carrying rings that are free to slide when the instrument is shaken. "Surmounting the frame of the sistrum," Plutarch notes, "is a carving of a cat with human features... The human face given to the cat is a sign of the intelligence and reason which govern the phases of the moon."

The cat goddess Bastet playing the sistrum. Egyptian bronze.

By placing the cat on one of the oldest of all musical instruments, which was used in the cults of Isis, Hathor, and Bastet, the Egyptian priests were honoring the enemy of the evil serpent, and the cat became the symbol of the sacred music whose rhythmic vibrations roused and alerted sleepers, while warding off evil spirits. The music inspired dancing, of which Bastet was again, appropriately, the goddess. The singer Cora Vaucaire once told me: "If I had been a dancer I think I would probably have given it up, after seeing a cat washing, which is grace itself," and many choreographers have drawn their inspiration from the cat's graceful movement.

The association of cats with music has not been confined to Egypt. The Javanese *saron* takes the form of a seated cat, while the Japanese went even further, literally making the cat into a musical instrument — the soundbox of the *samisen* used to have cat skin stretched across it, and cats' intestines were used to make the strings, just as catgut was later used in the West for the strings of violins.

Going from the sublime to the horrific, we must, regrettably, make mention of what has been variously known as cat music, *lamentatio catorum*, *musica de' gatti*, *Katzenmusik* or *concert miaulique*. This popular entertainment, recorded for posterity in various

engravings, consisted of tormenting cats for "musical" purposes, by shutting animals of both sexes and all ages in separate little cages, while tying their tails by cords to the keys of a kind of organ. As the "player" struck the keys, he drew howls of pain from the animals and roars of laughter from his depraved audience. One such performance, in Brussels in 1545, apparently gave great delight to Charles V and the future Philip II of Spain. Nobody's perfect...

With its sensitivity to "the well-tuned voice that tells the truth," the cat has often been an accomplice to music making. The eighteenth-century harpist Mlle. Dupuy described her cat as "my sternest critic"; and more recently Henri Sauguet, composer of *La Chatte*, performed by Serge Diaghilev's *Ballets Russes* in 1927, enjoyed seeing how his Siamese cats reacted to certain female singers whose voices were not always absolutely in tune. But this should not surprise us, for we know that cats can differentiate between semitones in the lower register and are even more sensitive to the higher frequencies.

Can a cat compose music? Domenico Scarlatti (1685–1757) certainly thought so, claiming to be indebted to his cat Pulcinella for the theme of his Fugue in G minor (L499) — one of his 555 sonatas for harpsichord — which he dedicated to the Infanta Maria Barbara of Spain, and left to posterity as the Cat Fugue. This is how Scarlatti described their collaboration:

My cat used to show a keen interest in the harpsichord. He would walk on the keys, going up and down from one end to the other. Sometimes he would pause longer on one note listening closely until the vibration ceased. One evening,

Charles-Antoine Coypel (1694–1752): engraving for The Cats, an opera by Antoinette Deshoulières.

while dozing in my armchair, I was roused by the sound of the harpsichord. My cat had started his musical stroll, and he really was picking out a melodic phrase. I had a sheet of paper to hand, and transcribed his composition.

Since then the cat has often been a source of inspiration for composers. Examples include Chopin's Cat Waltz (*Valse brillante in A minor* , opus 34), which is supposed to represent a cat playing with a ball of wool, and *Mi-a-ou*, from Gabriel Fauré's *Dolly* (1893), although here the meowing is just a distortion of "Messieu Aoul," the nickname that little Hélène Barlac gave to her brother Raoul.

Let us examine the various instruments used to suggest cats. The harpsichord, as we have seen, was chosen by Scarlatti, the piano by Chopin, and, utilizing four hands, by Fauré, as well as by Erik Satie (*Chanson du Chat*), Darius Milhaud (*Le Chat*, five pieces for piano), Henri Sauguet (for a setting of poems by Baudelaire), and Gabriel Pierné (*Trois Petits Chats Blancs*). The clarinet was used by Stravinsky in his *Berceuses du Chat* (four melodies for contralto and three clarinets, 1915), and the same instrument, in a lower register, represented the cat in Prokofiev's *Peter and the Wolf* (1936). Tchaikovsky, meanwhile, differentiates Puss-in-Boots and The White Cat in *The Sleeping Beauty* (1889), by means of expressive mewing from the woodwind, answered, *prestissimo*, by scratching and growling from the strings. For the

feline duet in Colette's *L'Enfant et les Sortilèges* (1925), Maurice Ravel chose to support the two voices (baritone and mezzo-soprano) with *glissandi* in the string section.

To list every instance of music relating to cats would require too much space. For the list of composers who have been inspired by cats is a long one indeed, from Offenbach, with *The Cat Who Was Transformed into a Woman* and *Dick Whittington and his Cat* to Claude Terrasse (*Puss-in-Boots*), and from Roberto de Simone (*The Cinderella Cat*, 1976) to Hans Werner Henze (*The English Cat*, 1984), not forgetting Andrew Lloyd Webber, whose musical, *Cats* was inspired by T.S. Eliot's *Old Possum's Book of Practical Cats*.

The art of the musical meow, which Ravel mastered so gloriously, already had two famous precedents. The first was Mozart's duet for soprano and baritone, *Nun, liebes Weibchen* (1790), where the meowing was contributed by the pen of Emmanuel Schikaneder, librettist of *The Magic Flute*. The most famous is, of course, the *Duetto buffo dei due gatti*, or *Cats' Duet*, that much loved party piece of many singers, which has traditionally been attributed to Rossini, but whose origins are, in fact, obscure, since most biographers of the composer doubt his authorship of the duet. Some are inclined to see it as a parody by G. Berthold of a theme from Rossini's *Otello*, others as a reworking of the *Kattecavatine* by the Danish composer Weyse. However, it could equally well have been a little entertainment improvised by Rossini for one of the musical *soirées* given at his home in the Rue de la Chaussée d'Antin in Paris.

We know that Rossini tended not to write down what he called his "sins of old age" unless he was short of money or under pressure from a publisher. Whatever the actual pedigree of the *Cats' Duet*, this delicious parody of the highly ornate *bel canto* style of singing, which was so much to the taste of nineteenth-century audiences, has enjoyed a brilliant career. Perhaps we should simply regard it as an anonymous work by an inspired alley cat. *Chi lo sa...*

Moritz von Schwind (1804–1871): Die Katzensymphonie (1868).

PLAYING THE CAT

"Cat and Mouse," "Cat on a Pole," "Cat's Cradle," "Puss in the Corner," "Tip-cat," "Cat-in-the-hole," "Chat-mimi-monté," "Gare au matou," "Gatta cieca"... Throughout history, children all over the world have played cat games. The ancient Egyptians had cat and mouse toys with moveable joints, and cats feature in numerous board games, card games, nursery rhymes, rounds, and riddles. But, as with many other traditional pastimes, there is often more to these cat games than meets the innocent eye.

"Cat and Rat" provides one instance: two children would face each other, blindfolded, both of them bound by a cord that was fixed to a point in the ground between them. The cat was armed with a stick, the rat with a sort of wooden saw that he had to wave around to reveal his presence. The cat pursued the rat, hitting him with the stick. The rat, who was not allowed to defend himself, had to announce his presence "musically" when the cat cried out "Rat!" Sometimes he accidentally came within reach of the cat's claws. The game finished after an appointed time, or when the rat cried for mercy.

Another game was "Cat and Mouse," a version of "Kiss in the Ring": the mouse was in the center of a circle; the cat, outside, tried to break through the barrier in order to steal a kiss from the mouse. This

*OPPOSITE **German "Felix the Cat" toy.***

sometimes led to erotic tumbles, but once the mouse had been "eaten," a new couple would start the game again. "The most amusing of games, and an ideal source of exercise," concluded Mme. Celnart, somewhat ingenuously, in her *Manuel des jeux de société* (Handbook of Party Games).

As if violence and sex were not enough, we can also detect an echo of sacrificial rites in "Cat!" and "Cat on a Pole." versions of the familiar game of "tag." A child chosen by lot has to pursue the other children, who climb walls, etc, to avoid being caught. The one who is seized takes the cat's place. Roger Caillois comments:

In this game, under the guise of childish innocence we can see the alarming election of a propitiatory victim or scapegoat: chosen by chance or by the meaningless, empty words of a counting rhyme, he is supposed to get rid of his taint by transmitting it, through touch, to the person he catches in the chase.

English children used to play "Cat's in the Cupboard," where one child stood, back turned, at some distance from the rest, who crept up, chanting "The cat's in the cupboard, and she can't see." Suddenly the cat turns and tries to catch one of them. Is it fanciful to suppose that this represents the cat-moon behaving treacherously? In some places hide-and-seek played in the dark is called "Cat's eyes," expressing the same idea of the all-seeing cat.

M A N E K I   N E K O . . .   G O O D   L U C K !

It seems almost certain that the cat was introduced into Japan as early as the sixth century A.D., probably from China or Korea. However, if the cat was originally an alien import, it is one of the few that the Japanese have taken to their hearts, boasting that in their bobtail cat, a tortoiseshell known as *mike neko*, they have the only breed on earth with a tail shaped like a chrysanthemum. As this strange creature is also credited with the power of warding off evil spirits, one can well understand the pride they take in it.

In the official Japanese version, the cat only came to Japan on the tenth day of the fifth month of the year 999. On that day, it is said, a Chinese mandarin presented the young emperor Idi-Jo (or Ichi-Jo) with a white female cat. When it gave birth to five kittens in the imperial palace of Kyoto, this evidence of fertility was taken to be an augury of a happy future for the cat. A thousand years later, the white cat reigns over industrial Japan, in the form of the *maneki neko*, a statuette of a tomcat, seated, with one paw raised. One sees examples of it everywhere, from the offices of the biggest companies and banks to the most humble shop or stall, and although the figurine looks like a child's toy, no one would dream of smiling in its presence.

But why all this respect? It is only a short step from fertility to prosperity, says the *maneki neko*, or

OPPOSITE **The maneki neko of Japan. Varnished terracotta (early twentieth century).**

"the cat that invites" — and that is the meaning of the famous gesture, tirelessly repeated by the charming cat in his formal pose, imbued with all the dignity of a national mascot. There is also a subtle distinction in its message: if the cat is raising its right paw, it is promising *fuku*, which means good luck and happiness; while the left paw ensures *sen ryo*, meaning lots of money. (The *ryo* was the gold currency of the Edo period from 1603 to 1867.) Needless to say, it is the

cat with upraised left paw that is the universal choice of commercial enterprises.

The origin of the *maneki neko* is somewhat obscure. One story has it that many years ago in Tokyo, in the pleasure district of Yoshiwara, a woman called O'Tsuna, the proprietress of a teahouse called the "Golden Cat" found herself short of money. Imprudently she accepted help from one of her customers, Hachiro Bei, but the money turned out to be stolen. Filled with remorse, the thief threw himself into the river Sumida, whereupon O'Tsuna realized that the crime had been committed for love of her, and impulsively she, too, leaped into the stream to join her suitor. This romantic piece of melodrama made such an impression on the general public that "The Golden Cat" enjoyed immense popularity, presumably under new ownership. From this story the merchant class of Tokyo concluded that association with cats brought good fortune.

There is another, equally poetic but less worldly explanation of the origin of the *maneki neko*, which we owe to the Buddhist monks of the Gotokuji, or Temple of Sublime Virtue, in the western part of Tokyo. At the time in question, more than 200 years ago, the Gotokuji was a minor temple, frequented only by the occasional pilgrim and the local inhabitants. One day a starving, exhausted cat appeared, and asked the monks for something to eat. Having been given its fill, the cat stayed with them, and from that day onward the temple prospered. The monks assumed the cat to be a messenger from heaven, and thereafter honored it as such in one of the sanctuaries of the temple.

At the Gotokuji today there is still an immense statue of the *maneki neko*, with a friendly smile, beside the effigy of the Buddha, and visitors to the temple ring the bell, burn incense, and pray before it. Far from the arcane world of high finance or the hurly-burly of the marketplace, the holy cat at the Gotokuji is simply the protector of children and guardian of the spirits of the dead. The comical silhouette of the *maneki neko*, endlessly repeated in row upon row of votive statuettes, makes a cheerful and colorful contrast with the rigorous Zen solemnity of the Buddhist cemetery.

After suffering hundreds of years of hatred and massacre at the hands of Europeans, the cat has at last won back some of the homage it deserves. Aided, no doubt, by its attractive appearance and civilized habits — Louis Pasteur was particularly impressed by its cleanliness — by the end of the nineteenth century it was firmly established as a favorite household pet. All that remained was to celebrate feline beauty in ceremonies to match the splendors of Pharaonic Egypt.

Cat mania originated in Great Britain in July 1871, when an aesthete — an avid horticulturalist and animal lover named Harrison Weir — had the idea of organizing a cat exhibition at Crystal Palace, London. The event was a great success, with a crowd of visitors coming to admire the 160 cats on show. Many cat competitions were to follow, their popularity spreading worldwide, while clubs and associations in the hundreds sprang up to cater to the new enthusiasts.

Universally praised for its beauty, the cat had become a favorite subject for several artists; the next step, obviously, was to gain entry into the museums. This happened on June 12, 1982, when the first cat museum opened its doors to the public near Basle in Switzerland. The event was greeted by the press without even a trace of ridicule as if, suddenly, it

Molds for "langues de chats." Katzenmuseum, Riehen, Switzerland.

seemed perfectly acceptable to honor the memory of the divine descendants of Bastet.

Since then, other museums have been opened, in Amsterdam and in eastern France (addresses are given on p.116). Their documents, artifacts, and works of art bear witness to the importance of the cat in our daily lives and in our imagination, proof, if proof were needed, that at the dawn of the second millennium, man's relationship with the cat has changed from that of merciless torturer to willing and contented slave. A fitting regression, and one about which we will hear no complaints from the cats.

CAT MUSEUMS

KATZENMUSEUM
Baselstrasse 101
4124 RIEHEN – BS
Switzerland
Tel: 061 672694/2619323

MUSÉE DU CHAT
Rue de l'Église
70800 AINVELLE
France
Tel: 84 49 89 19

KATTENKABINET
Herengracht 468
1017 CA AMSTERDAM
The Netherlands
Tel: 20 6265378

SELECT BIBLIOGRAPHY

Juliet Clutton-Brock, *The British Museum Book of Cats*, The Trustees of the British Museum, London, 1988.

Fred Gettings, *The Secret Lore of the Cat*, Grafton Books, London, 1989.

Herodotus, *The Histories*, tr. A. de Selincourt, Penguin, London, 1971.

Mildred Kirk, *The Everlasting Cat*, Faber & Faber, London, 1977.

Fernand Méry, *The Life, History and Magic of the Cat*, tr. Emma Street, Paul Hamlyn, London, 1967.

John P. O'Neill, *Metropolitan Cats*, Harry N. Abrams/The Metropolitan Museum of Modern Art, New York, 1981.

Plutarch, *De Iside et Osiride*, ed J. G. Griffiths, University of Wales, Cardiff, 1970.

John Sharkey, *Celtic Mysteries*, Thames & Hudson, London, 1975.

Dorothy Margaret Stuart, *A Book of Cats: Literary, Legendary and Historical*, Methuen, London, 1959.

BREEDS OF THE CATS ILLUSTRATED

Front cover Bombay
p.6   Chartreux
p.10   Birman (Sacred Cat of Burma)
p.11   Long-haired black
p.12   Russian blue
p.13   Long-haired colorpoint
p.14   Domestic cat
p.16   Long-haired colorpoint
p.20   Domestic cat
p.21   Wildcat (*felis silvestris*)
p.22   Birman
p.23   Long-haired blue cream
p.24   Birman
p.25   Venetian Soriano
p.26   Tabby pointed Siamese
p.29   Foreign white
p.30   Domestic cat
p.35   Birman
p.39   Somali
p.42   Selkirk Rex
p.44   Norwegian forest cat
p.47   Russian blue
p.49   Long-haired golden
p.51   Bombay
p.53   Domestic cat
p.54   Domestic cat
p.55   Selkirk Rex
p.56   Seal point Siamese
p.57   Domestic cat
p.58   Birman
p.59   Abyssinian
p.61   Domestic cat
p.62   Balinese (young subject)
p.64   Birman
p.65   Long-haired colorpoint
p.66   Long-haired chocolate
p.67   Balinese (young subject)
p.68   Sphinx
p.70   British blue
p.74   Long-haired blue
p.76   American curl
p.77   Chartreux

p.78   Chartreux
p.80   Devon Rex
p.81   Devon Rex
p.82   British silver spotted tabby
p.84   California spangled cat
p.86   Bombay
p.87   Long-haired blue
p.88   Long-haired chinchilla
p.89   Long-haired chinchilla
p.92   British red tabby
p.93   Scottish Fold
p.94   Balinese
p.95   Long-haired red
p.100 Burmilla
p.101 Birman
p.102 Foreign blue
p.103 Long-haired chinchilla
p.104 Angora
p.108 Angora
p.113 Scottish Fold
p.114 Long-haired chinchilla